MASTERING THE ART
OF INSTRUCTION

The 9 Essential Instructional Skills
Every Teacher Needs to Master

ISRAEL GALINDO

Published by Educational Consultants

CONTENTS

INTRODUCTION 4

Chapter 1: Instruction and Learning 8

Chapter 2: The Stages of Learning

               Through Instruction 13

Chapter 3: How to Use Learning Objectives 26

Chapter 4: How to Begin Instruction 38

Chapter 5: Using Induction to Carry the Lesson 46

Chapter 6: How To Ask Effective Questions 51

Chapter 7: How To Respond to Student Responses 59

Chapter 8: How to Maintain Attention 66

Chapter 9: How To Teach A Concept 82

Chapter 10: How To Teach A Principle 88

Chapter 11: How to End Instruction 92

Bibliography 100

Introduction

Instruction is probably the most widely used approach in the educational enterprise in schools, churches, and business. You are so familiar with instruction that you can instantly recognize it when you see it. You enter a room (usually called a "classroom"), and you see a podium where the "teacher" will stand. You see the chairs or tables arranged in a certain configuration and you immediately intuit that is where the "students" will sit. Looking around the room you can see where the "focus of attention" will be—toward the front of the room where the teacher is and from where learning will flow. Even if there is no one in the room the arrangement of the space tells you immediately that "instruction happens here."

This book is about mastering the art of instruction. Instruction is a narrow slice of what we call teaching, and an even narrower slice of what we mean when we use the term education. As educators we engage in an enterprise that is deeper and wider than the singular acts, skills, and functions of teaching and instruction. Education involves nurture, inspiration, formation, relationship, love, philosophy, and a number of other broad concerns. Teaching also involves a set of deeper and broader concerns, like philosophy, ethics, relationship, ethos, culture, theory, methodology, ideology, and epistemology. But when we talk about instruction, the focus of this book, we are talking about a specific pedagogy of teaching. This is an important distinction, because while instruction is an effective means to facilitate learning, it should not be equated with what constitutes teaching in its entirety.

Having said that, we want to appreciate that instruction is a powerful act. Instruction is highly teacher-dependent in terms of whether or not how we teach will effectively translate to meaningful learning on the part of the learner. In fact, in order to help facilitate learning, a teacher must understand that how he or she practices instruction can either enhance or hinder learning in the classroom environment. That's an important point, so here it is again: depending on how a teacher engages in instruction, he or she can enhance learning or inhibit learning in the classroom setting. In other words, when it comes to effective instruction, how you do it matters. For the purpose of this book, we can define Instruction as the intentional didactic practices of the teacher in the classroom setting that helps bring about learning on the part of the student.

It is no accident that the teacher is at the front of the room in the classroom setting. The reason for that is that in the instructional setting, effective learning is very dependent on the function of the teacher. Research has demonstrated that in the instructional setting, effective learning happens to the extent that the teacher engages in sound instructional teaching functions. So here is the frightful truth: depending on how you practice certain basic instructional acts, you are either helping your students learn or you are actually inhibiting their ability to learn. Again, how you teach matters. Do it correctly, and your students learn; do it poorly and your students suffer.

For those who teach in the classroom environment, this truth remains: of all other factors in the teaching-learning experience, it is the teacher's ability to teach effectively that makes the difference in whether or not meaningful learning happens. For those of us who are called to teach in the congregational setting, this insight is critical.

On any given Sunday morning, the average Sunday School teacher has at best, forty minutes of instructional time during which to engage in Bible study and impart important truth. By instructional time we mean time actually spent on the teaching-learning act. Instructional time does not include, entering the classroom, getting coffee, chatting and fellowship, passing around the student quarterlies, taking prayer requests, taking attendance, dealing with interruptions, and all of the other things that go on during a Sunday School class. So, a good teacher has, at best, forty minutes for a lesson. For the majority of students in that class, those forty minutes will be the extent of their formal Christian Education experience during the week. Compare that to the number of hours that the student in your Sunday School class will spend watching television during the week (and you can be assured that they also are learning something from watching television!).

So, given that on any given Sunday you have at most forty minutes of instructional time, and given the insight that depending on how you, as the teacher, go about engaging in the instructional act you are either enhancing of inhibiting learning in your students, are you now aware of how critical it is to know how practice essential instructional skills correctly? Similarly, in a formal school context, the number of hours of actual instructional time in an average class is less than three hours a day, even though students often are at school for seven or more hours — and that's on a good day.

The instructional process presented in this book is research-based, not faddish advice. This is not an uncritical advocacy of a particular "teaching style" based on personal predilection. The two primary sources that inform the concepts and practices in the book are research in the field of classroom instruction and current research into learning and the brain. Research in classroom instruction has identified one hundred and twenty-one specific teacher behaviors that directly relate to increased student learning and supportive classroom behavior. In this book you will learn nine of those specific essential instructional skills. We will focus on these nine because they are the most essential of the instructional acts used in teaching that influence learning positively. The nine skills span the arc from the beginning to end of the instructional experience. Other important instructional skills will be introduces along the way. If you master these nine instructional skills, and if you practice them in the way that enhances learning rather than inhibits learning, you will be on your way to being an effective teacher who can deliver powerful and meaningful learning to your students.

Instruction is a pedagogy. It is a systematic way of teaching informed by educational principles of pedagogy and research from the field of education. In this book we'll present the nine essential instructional skills every teacher needs to master. Those nine skills are: designing learning objectives, starting instruction, using induction, asking instructional questions, managing student responses, maintaining student attention, teaching concepts, teaching principles, and ending the instructional experience through closure.

Chapter 1

Instruction and Learning

Instruction is the most frequently used approach to teaching. So much so that most of us identify learning with instruction when in reality, they are two sides of the same coin—but two distinct sides nevertheless. Used correctly, instruction can be one of the most effective ways of teaching. However, after decades of training teachers, my observation is that most teachers do not know how to use instruction as a way of teaching in ways that can be effective. This is true of teachers in professional settings (university campuses and theological schools) and in a volunteer context, like a church education program.

The fact is that instruction is a particular educational approach, a pedagogy, that must be applied rigorously if it is to be effective. The "stand and deliver" method (the lecture) that most untrained teachers seem to use (and many professional teachers seem to favor) rarely translates to effective learning on the part of the student. The problem is that lecture is not instruction. Lecture is a method intended to convey information, while instruction is a systematic educational approach intended to bring about learning. Even when teachers follow prepared teaching plans, a lack of understanding about the dynamics of teaching and learning in the classroom, with a failure to understand what instruction is, how it works, and how its application brings about student learning means that most teachers will not do much beyond going through the motions of teaching while failing to instruct. Effective instruction follows universal processes regardless of the context, regardless of the content, regardless of the personality of the teacher and regardless of secondary concerns such as student "learning styles."

Research into effective classroom instruction has identified one hundred and twenty-one specific teacher instructional behaviors that help facilitate learning. Further, research has demonstrated two things: (1) these specific teacher instructional behaviors have a direct correlation on how the brain learns, and (2) the way a teacher performs these behaviors is critical. Done correctly these teaching behaviors enhance learning in the instructional setting. Done inappropriately, or failing to do them, a teacher actually inhibits learning in the instructional setting. Covering all one hundred and twenty-one of those teacher instructional behaviors is outside of the scope of this book. Some of the one hundred and twenty-one acts relate to planning, evaluation, and classroom management. While those are important, we'll not focus on those aspects of instruction. Our attention will be on teacher instructional performance in the classroom setting during a teaching session. In presenting the nine essential instructional skills, we will combine several of these specific behaviors into "sets" that you, the teacher, can easily incorporate so as to become more effective instructors.

The Four Components of Instruction

Before we examine the nine essential instructional skills in the following chapters, let's get the big picture about instruction.

The practice of instruction has four components: outcome (what the students will learn and why), content (what you will teach), process (consisting of two facets, how you, the teacher instructs, and how the learner acquires learning), and context (the location and environment in which learning takes place). The decisions you, the teacher, must make, therefore, are about what you will teach, how you need to teach it, what you want to see happen at the end of the instructional session, and what is the best environment for learning. The clearer you are about these four components before you begin instruction the more effective will be your teaching.

Instructional OUTCOME refers to the desired result of the instructional experience. An outcome can be in the form of cognitive behaviors like understanding or comprehending, affective actions like appreciating or valuing, or a skill or product that students create. Outcomes need to be intentional and overt because they are the means by which students demonstrate what they have learned and the extend to which they have learned. Outcomes reveal whether students can apply what they have learned both in the classroom, and beyond. One outcome question is, can students solve problems and take action based on what they have learned? In Chapter 2 you will learn how to create effective instructional outcomes.

CONTENT refers to what you will teach, that is, what you want your students to know or know how to do. The content of instruction typically falls under three categories: concepts, principles, and skills. In this book we will primarily focus on concepts and principles, since those are most often the concern of classroom instruction. The teaching of skills has its own particular educational concerns and often is accomplished through other means alongside of instruction like coaching, apprenticeship, and training. Of necessity, skills need to be taught and acquired in the contexts in which they will be used, normally outside of the classroom—a playing field or a professional setting, for example. Because educational processes need to be applied rigorously if they are to be effective, it's important to use the appropriate educational approach to the type of learning outcome we want to see students acquire. When we neglect to do this we often engage in what I call "pretend learning," which means we use educational methods to teach things they are not meant to teach and then "pretend" that students are actually learning what we want them to learn. To use some common examples: you can't teach someone to swim in a classroom setting through instruction, and you can't teach someone to dribble a basketball by having them read about it in a book. Those skills need to be taught using non-instructional methods, like coaching and drill, in the environment in which the skills will be applied.

PROCESS refers to the learning activities and methods you use in instruction that will help your student acquire understanding and comprehension of the content. The process of instruction will vary depending on two things: (1) the readiness and ability level of the students who make up the class, and (2) the desired outcome of the instructional session. There is an endless number to the variety of educational methods one can use by way of process. However, the most important thing to keep in mind is that "process determines outcome." The methods that you choose by way of instructional process must be congruent with the outcome you are after. Methods are not ends in and of themselves; they are of value only to the extent that they help your students achieve the learning outcomes you've set out to realize. In short, learning methods must match and support learning outcomes. Process in the instructional context also refers to the way you teach, and that includes using the nine essential instructional skills appropriately. Process also includes following the five stages of instruction rigidly and intentionally.

The fourth educational component that influences teaching and learning is CONTEXT. This component is perhaps the most underappreciated of the four. The context of the teaching-learning experience influences all aspects of both teaching and learning in ways we tend to underestimate. Teaching in the context of a college classroom is different than teaching in the context of a workplace training workshop. Teaching in a congregation is different than teaching in the context of a theological school. Teaching in the context of a lifelong learning program, whose goal is enrichment, is different than in a for-credit degree granting program, whose goal is preparation or certification.

It seems not uncommon for teachers and instructors to fail in considering the importance of context when preparing and leading an educational program or leading a class. Context frames everything in a teaching-learning experience, from outcomes to didactic approaches. While instruction is an applicable and suitable approach to teaching in any context, how it must be applied is informed by the context itself.

❖

Chapter 2

The Stages of Learning
Through Instruction

Just like a good story, instruction has a narrative arch: beginning, middle, and end. If you leave out one of those parts of a narrative, you have an incomplete and unsatisfying story. The same is true with instruction: leave out any one stage of the instructional act and you have an unsatisfying learning experience (and possibly, an ineffective one). Instruction achieves meaningful learning in a predictable five-stage sequence. The stages of instruction are the same regardless of what content you are teaching, what learning activities (methods) you will use, what learning outcomes you are seeking on the part of the student, or the ages of your students. The five stages are:

1. Preparation for Learning

2. Concept Acquisition

3. Deep Understanding and Comprehension

4. Memory Formation

5. Functional Integration.

An easier way to remember the five stages of instruction is:

1. Prepare

2. Acquire

3. Understand

4. Remember

5. Apply.

Preparation for Learning

There are three things you need to know about the brain when it comes to learning. First, the brain's "Job 1" is survival. This is such a powerful purpose for your brain that it will willingly sacrifice other parts of your body to ensure its survival. You may have read or heard about the amazing story of 27-year-old hiker Aron Ralston. Hiking his way through a 3-foot-wide section of Utah's Blue John Canyon, Ralston had no warning before the giant boulder shifted onto him, pinning his right arm in a crack in the canyon wall. His water ran out after four days. On the sixth day he came to the chilling realization that there was only one way he could survive. Using a pocketknife, Ralston cut off his own arm, rappelled sixty feet to the canyon floor and then walked through the rough landscape till he found help and rescue.

Upon hearing that story most of us find it incomprehensible how someone could take such a drastic measure, even when survival is at stake. But a neuro-psychologist would likely respond by saying, "Yes, that makes perfect sense. The brain felt its survival was threatened and knew it could live on without an arm, so it said, 'Cut it off and get me out of here.'"

Related to learning, the amazing thing seems to be that the brain will invest energy in things that ensure its "existential survival" once the basic physical needs are met. This may be the reason why education can have such intrinsic motivation for some people—it is a way to ensure future survival. This idea is consistent with Abraham Maslow's theory of human motivation, now commonly referred to as Maslow's Hierarchy of Needs (Maslow, "A Theory of Human Motivation," 1943, Psychological Review, 50, 370-396). He contended that as humans meet 'basic needs', they seek to satisfy successively 'higher needs' that make up a set hierarchy. Usually depicted in the form of a pyramid hierarchy, the stages of needs go from "lower" to "higher." Maslow identified Deficiency Needs: physiological, safety, love/belonging, esteem; and Growth Needs: Self-Actualization; Self-Transcendence.

The second thing you need to know about the brain is that it seeks patterns and connections. If the brain cannot recognize or create a pattern for what it is experiencing it cannot make meaning of the experience. If the brain cannot quickly or easily connect new experiences (and learning is an experience for the brain) with existing patterns in its neural network, then it will not expend the energy to retain the new information—it's too busy expending energy for Job 1: survival. Simply put, the learner will not learn what she does not understand.

Preparation for learning in the instructional setting is merely a way to pre-dispose the brain for learning and retaining new information into its neural network. Much of this happens on an unconscious level in the student, but must be done intently by the instructor. When you prepare your students for learning you in effect "set" the brain for the experience of instruction. This "setting" is the way the brain provides for itself a frame of reference for receiving and interpreting the information it is about to receive. Imagine you go to a movie theatre. You go to the concession counter and buy some popcorn and soda, then make your way into the theatre. As soon as you enter the room your brain recognizes the environment. You sit down on the comfortable high-back seat, put your drink in the cupholder and stare at the large projection screen at the front of the room.

Likely there are previews running before the main feature starts. At this point you brain starts to "set" itself for the experience to come. Your brain engages in an internal dialogue and is saying to itself, "Ah, I recognize this, it's a movie theater. I know what kind of information I'll be receiving (visual and auditory, images and emotions) and I know how to receive it and interpret it. Let me "set" myself for it. I see that I don't really have to 'pay attention' yet because the previews are playing and the movie hasn't started. I'll wait in anticipation for the cues that the movie is about to begin before I pay attention."

Now imagine that you walk into a classroom. Your brain takes in the environment and says to itself, "Ah, I recognize this context, it's a classroom. I know what kind of information I'll be receiving, and know how to look and listen for it. I'll "set" myself for that kind of information and will look for the cues I need. I see that the teacher is fiddling around with his notes and equipment, so I don't have to pay attention yet. I'll wait for the cues that tell me that instruction has begun." Your brain does this every time it enters an environment where information is coming its way. You experience this set when you enter a classroom, a movie theatre, a church, or an airport.

An effective instructor helps the brain "set" itself for receiving instructional information and for engaging in the learning experience through specific instructional acts. One example such an instructional act is called an "advance organizer." We'll examine different ways to provide advance organizers in Chapter 3. When you prepare for learning by helping the students' brains "set," by providing advance organizers or other means, you help make subsequent learning proceed more quickly.

The greater the amount of preparation stimulus, the more the brain is able to extract, organize, and "compartmentalize" the information. The brain puts new information into a short-term memory "buffer zone" for rapid access (or, for you computer buffs, into "RAM," Random Access Memory). If the information is not reinforced and used over time, it simply lays unconnected and random. Ultimately, the brain will not retain that information because it will not exert the energy it takes to maintain random unconnected pieces of date—after all, the brain's Job 1 is survival, and it will put more of its energy into that than into maintaining meaningless trivia, that is, information not perceived as important to its survival.

One of the key characteristics of the cortex, important to learning, is the ability to detect and create patterns of meaning. This process involves deciphering cues and making connections. Ultimately, learning is the development of goal-oriented neural networks. Single brain cells (neurons) aren't smart, but integrated groups of neurons that fire together, on cue, to re-create purposeful patterns, are. Learning happens when elaborate networks are created over time through the process of: making initial connections; developing the right connections; and strengthening connections. This complex and beautiful process begins with the first step: preparation for learning.

Concepts Acquisition

The first stage of instruction is preparation for learning, followed by concept acquisition. In this stage learners are introduced to a concept, a principle, or to selected information that makes up the content of study. What is important to understand about this stage of instruction is that a concept is a particular thing that must be taught a particular way in the instructional setting in order for the student to be able to acquire it.

Finally, in order for content information to be more than trivia, the instructor must be able to choose content that leads to meaningful learning. Some information is more important than others—and some information leads to meaningful learning while other is merely trivia.

How many times has this happened to you? You studied long and hard for an exam at school. You review notes, memorize lists of facts, organize an outline of information, and read and re-read parts of the text in preparation for test. Fueled by the motivation of anxiety you show up for class, complete the test, turn it in and walk out the door, relieved that one more exam is over with. And then, you realize that ten minutes after the exam you can't remember much of what you wrote, the questions that were asked, or anything that you "learned" during a long night of cramming.

Frustrated, you wonder why there is so little return on investment for all the time, energy, and anxiety you put into memorizing information for an exam. One simple answer is that in terms of learning, you likely focused on information and not on concept acquisition. Therefore, the information was little more than trivia and not worth retaining after the limited "application" of what you learned: an information dump on an exam. And, since Job 1 for the brain is survival, your brain was happy to dump all that information on a piece of paper and leave it there rather than extent the energy it takes to retain disconnected facts and information. Effective teachers know how to identify and choose meaningful content that will result in meaningful learning. As we will see in Chapters 9 and 10, the most meaningful kinds of information are concepts and principles.

What this means for you as an instructor is to never confuse sharing information with learning. The neurological definition of concept acquisition is the formation of new synaptic connections—the stage when neurons "talk" to one another and make a connection. The simplest expression of this principle is the old adage of going from the known to the unknown. If you want to teach a person something "new," then you have to connect it with something "old"—something they already know.

Effective instruction literally is an act of changing the brain by causing the learner to graft new neuronal patterns onto existing ones. Specifically, if you are to help your students learn, then you need to connect new learning with the existing neural networks in the student. This simple and powerful principle highlights the connection between the first stage of instruction, preparation for learning, with the second step of concept acquisition. Preparation for learning provides learners with a foundation upon which to build connections. The more connections you help provide, the better and faster learning will occur. The more the learners know before you begin formal instruction, the better they will be able to engage in acquiring meaningful concepts.

Deep Understanding and Comprehension

An enormous gap often exists between what the teacher explains and what the learner understands. Good teachers work at ensuring that this does not happen. To reduce this gap, teachers need to use the rigorous process of instruction to engage students for deep understanding. This is accomplished through the use of direct instruction and interactive learning strategies. Comprehension is the ability to understand the meaning or importance of something—to know why something is so. Testing for comprehension, assessing misunderstanding, and making corrections as we work through the process of instruction is a critical approach to teaching with the brain in mind.

Confusion is the biggest obstacle to learning: a student cannot learn what he or she does not understand. Once a learner is lost in confusion, the brain somehow switches off. Because the brain is stingy about its energy use it will just not put out the amount of energy required to "figure something out" unless there is a goal-oriented purpose to the activity. This pattern can be recognized early in a person's development.

If you observe a small child at play you will see that the child will remain engaged until he or she becomes confused by something—at that point, he or she will literally turn away. That pattern continues to hold true in the instructional setting with students of any age. Watch for it: as soon as your students become confused by something you do or say, they'll turn away and stop "paying attention." The effective instructor learns to adjust the teaching-learning process to avoid confusion, to maintain attention, to test for comprehension, and to correct misunderstanding.

The brain is very efficient about creating synaptic connections as it processes information and experiences. These connections are stored in short-term memory, but they are stored temporarily, and then lost, unless additional neural connections are made. Neural space is expensive and making connections takes energy and the brain is most concerned with saving that which is important for survival. To ensure that the brain maintains the synaptic connections made from new learning, additional intention through elaboration, rehearsal, and practice is necessary. This leads to what we mean by "deep understanding." Understanding is the ability to use knowledge in different contexts and in new and novel ways. The evidence of understanding is application and creativity: being able to use what you know in different contexts and in a variety of ways.

Memory Formation

Even with plenty of opportunity for being exposed to content, experimentation, and interaction, it is still not enough to ensure memory formation in the student. Memory formation — putting concepts into long-term, permanent memory is what facilitates meaningful learning. After all, you cannot use what you can't remember. You cannot apply knowledge to new situations if you cannot access it. Therefore, an important stage in the instructional process is to work at ensuring memory formation.

Some of the factors that contribute to the issue of memory (retrievability) include: adequate rest (brain breaks), emotional connection, context, nutrition, quality and quantity of associations with past experiences and knowledge, the learner's stage of development, learner states (relaxed, anxious, and bored), and prior learning experiences. Some of these are out of the control of the teaching in the instructional setting—but many of them can be, and need to be, addressed if instruction is to be effective. As we will see in subsequent chapters, teachers have powerful resources to facilitate memory formation during instruction: repetition, rehearsal, cues, emotional response, association, reinforcement, etc. For the moment we want to stress this important point: memory formation is a necessary stage in effective instruction and must not be skipped.

Functional Integration

The final stage of the instructional process is functional integration. Functional integration is merely a fancy term for what we mean by "application." Recall that our basic definition of what constitutes understanding is the ability to use knowledge in different contexts and in new ways. Instruction does not end until the student is given the opportunity to apply what he or she has learned. Fortunately, application happens on many levels, and in many domains, from actual to simulation, from cognitive to emotional, from physical to abstract. For example, you can ask students to apply what they have learned by demonstrating in real time how it is actually done, or by creating a diagram that depicts how it might be done. You can ask students to apply knowledge by manipulating a real object or by explaining how they would manipulate that object given a certain set of conditions under a certain set of circumstances.

The resource that the teacher has in this stage has to do with a rather amazing and quirky truth about the brain. One of the most amazing insights related to how the brain works is that the brain cannot distinguish and external reality from an internal reality. As far as the brain is concerned an imagined experience inside the mind is as "real" as an actual experience in the physical world. Our brains have mechanisms to protect us from potentially harmful implications of this fact.

The most dramatic evidence of this phenomenon tends to come from persons with organic brain syndromes where the typical corrections, frames of reference, and safety features cause persons to be unable to distinguish internal and external realities. But for most of us, our brains serve us well in helping us make that distinction and protecting us from the consequences of the phenomena. For example, when we sleep our brain in effect immobilizes our bodies lest we start running around when our mind dreams it's running around (though I must admit that I've awoken sweating and breathing hard from nightmares and once woke up with the taste of vanilla on my tongue after dreaming I was eating ice cream!).

Some persons have learned to exploit the inability of the brain to distinguish an internal reality from an external one. Whether experiencing something or thinking about experiencing it, the brain fires off brain cells and creates pathways and patterns of connectivity—in effect, it learns. A common practice among athletes is to go over and over in their imagination a skill or behavior. As they think through a perfect throw or a perfect drive the brain rehearses these (internal) actions, creating patterns of learning that later are repeated and reinforced in the physical world. What this all means for instruction and learning is that a teacher can "create an experience" for application in the classroom by using techniques like simulation, pretending, and imagination.

Functional integration (application of knowledge) is the evidence of understanding. When a teacher reaches this stage of the instructional process he or she is asking students to demonstrate their ability to use knowledge in different contexts and in new ways. The specific way in which students will demonstrate functional integration will relate directly to the learning objectives of the instruction. In this way, instruction ends where it begins. You end instruction by realizing in practice what you set out at the start as a goal.

Summary

Before we move on to examine the specifics of our instructional repertoire, the nine essential instructional skills, let's review the big picture about instruction. Instruction is a particular approach to teaching that must be done in a particular way. In order for educational processes to be effective, they must be applied rigorously. This is true of instruction as a facet of teaching. Instruction consists of three components: outcomes, content, process, and context. Further, there are five distinct stages to every instructional event. Below is a chart that summarizes the five stages of instruction with corresponding examples of what the instructor does, and what the student does during each stage.

The nine essential instructional skills covered in the following chapters correlate directly with this classic five-stage instructional process and give attention to how the brain learns.

In this chapter we've looked at some general concepts about instruction. Here are the main points:

- Instruction is a specific way of teaching that requires rigorous attention to its particular educational process. There are one hundred and twenty-one specific instructional acts.
- The most effective practice of instruction gives attention to how the brain actually learns.

- Our focus on instruction in this book will be primarily on teaching concepts and principles, though skills acquisition can also be a part of instruction.

- There are four components to instruction: outcomes, content, process, and context. Instructional methods must be congruent with both content type and desired learning outcomes.

- There are five stages in the instructional process: Preparation, Concept Acquisition, Deep Understanding and Comprehension, Memory Formation, Functional Integration (or, Prepare, Acquire, Understand, Remember, Apply).

What the Instructor Does	What the Student Does
1. Preparation	
"Sets" the student's mind for learning by priming, pre-exposure to content, advance organizers. Shares overt learning outcomes.	Prepares for learning, focuses on the instructional experience, sets a mental and emotional frame of reference for receiving instruction.
2. Concept Acquisition	
Presents content (concepts and principles) through explication, direct and indirect instruction.	Listens, interprets, and makes connections with previous knowledge. Engages in learning activities.
3. Deep Understanding and Comprehension	
Tests for comprehension, performs error correction, explication in depth, provides learning methods for content interpretation.	Listens, explains, interprets; participates in learning activities, assesses self for comprehension and corrects misunderstandings.
4. Memory Formation	
Reinforces content acquisition through review, rest ("brain breaks"), emotional response, associations, encoding learning, practice, rehearsal	Commits learning to memory and makes affective connection. Participates in learning activities for reinforcement, encoding, practice, rehearsal, and interpretation.
5. Functional Integration	
Verifies achievement of learning outcomes (learning) through extended usage, application, and engages in closure.	Applies knowledge and demonstrates understanding. Demonstrates achievement of outcomes. Engages in emotional closure.

❖

Chapter 3

How to Use Learning Objectives

In my work with faculty members I often review course syllabi. It's not uncommon for their syllabi to lack published learning outcomes. Or, if there's a section for "learning outcomes," the list describes what the teacher wants to do, rather than identify the outcome of what the learner will learn. It's always surprising how hard it is for some teachers to answer the question, "But what do you want your students to learn or be able to do?"

A second question that stumps teachers related to learning outcomes is, "Can you tell me how these learning outcomes align with the program or degree goals in which this course is situated?" Unless there are institutional programmatic guidelines to course and syllabus design, it seems most teachers fail to think about how their teaching goals, and student learning outcomes, align with the intended purpose and goal of the educational program in which they teach. That this is an impediment to effective teaching and learning is self-evident.

Learning objectives are the set of principles, concepts, procedures, and skills you want your learners to learn by the end of the course, unit, or lesson. Having a clear idea about these objectives gives you direction in constructing your syllabus, defining performance criteria, creating assessment rubrics, and deciding which teaching strategies and learning experiences will help bring about the desired learning. The more concretely you can define these objectives, the more easily you can assess how well your students are learning.

While writing effective learning objectives has great educational value, there are some challenges in doing so. For one thing, it takes time to develop effective learning objectives. It's a hard starting place because it requires thinking. And, to be honest, it requires more thinking than most teachers put into preparing for their teaching experiences, whether it's a course or a lesson.

Investing in the hard work of creating and using effective learning objectives is worth it because they help you define the educational goals of your course, unit, or lesson. Crafting effective learning objectives will help point you toward appropriate methods, learning experience, and materials that will help your students learn what you intend for them to learn. In addition, when you write an effective learning objective, it will define for you and for your learners how you will know that learning has been achieved.

Writing and using learning objectives will make your course, or lesson, a much more effective learning experience for your students. For one thing, learning objectives provide the greatest defense in accountability. Your published learning objectives, along with well-designed assessment rubrics and practices, will demonstrate the effectiveness of your teaching. This is an increasingly important issue in today's educational environments.

Additionally, learning objectives make it easier to evaluate student learning. Theoretically, your published learning objectives can be the final exam you will use to test your learners. As such, this helps keep your teaching on target, since you (and your learners) are clear about the scope and direction of the course or lesson. Publishing your learning objectives lets learners know where the course is going and what has to be done to get there.

Taking the time to write effective learning objectives makes it easier to design your learning experience. Once you determine what you want your students to learn by the end of the course, you can make more informed choices about the methods you need to use to get them there.

Finally, writing effective learner outcomes enables others to help you in determining the value of what you are teaching. Sharing your learning objectives with others, especially with students, can help you decide whether or not what you want to teach has sufficient value for the learners. This is important for adult learners especially, because they are more selective about the potential "return on investment" of their time and energy.

Formulating Instructional Objectives

There are three key terms you'll need to know in order to write effective learning objectives: behavior, terminal behavior, and criterion.

Behavior: Any visible or measurable activity displayed by a learner. (Example: "The student will begin a story with a dramatic introduction.")

Terminal behavior: The behavior that the learner is to demonstrate after the learning experience. (Example: "The student will tell a story using effective storytelling techniques.")

Criterion: The standard by which the terminal behavior is evaluated to determine if learning has occurred. (Example: "When telling a story, the student will use three of the five dramatic voices of storytelling.").

Make Your Learning Objectives Meaningful

Merely writing learning objectives correctly is insufficient in making for an effective learning experience. Learning is effective only when it is meaningful to the learner. In order for a learning objective to be meaningful it must convey your intent, and be written from the standpoint of the learner (that is, it must communicate what the learner will learn, not what you, the instructor, will do).

Second, a meaningful learning objective will be as specific as possible. The single weakest way to write a learning objective is to write it so broad as to be meaningless (and this is the single greatest fault of most learning objectives). Often, this is related to the tendency to attempt too much content coverage in a course or a lesson. An objective that states, "The student will learn to tell a story," is too vague to be helpful to you or to your learner. For example, it does no communicate what kind of story the student will learn to tell; how well you expect the student to tell it; nor what storytelling skills the student will learn.

Similarly, a learning objective that reads, "The student will learn about the history preceding the Second World War," is too broad and too vague. It leaves the learner asking, "Learn what "about" that history?" "Will I learn ALL of history before WWII?!" Effective learning objectives specify the outcome enough so the student can read your objective and say, "Oh, I know exactly what I'm going to learn!"

Writing Meaningful Objectives

In order to write an effective meaningful learning objective, you need to: (1) write it from the standpoint of the learner, (2) identify the terminal behavior, (3) describe the conditions under which the behavior should occur, and (4) specify the criteria for acceptable performance.

1. Identify the terminal behavior.

What do you want the student to be able to do?

What do you want the student to be able to do at the end of your course?

What do you want the student to be able to do at the end of a unit of study?

What do you want the student to be able to do at the end of a lesson?

2. Define the behavior by describing the conditions under which the behavior should occur.

When and where do you want the student to be able to do it?

3. Specify the criteria of acceptable performance.

How well must the student be able to do it?

The Terminal Behavior

The terminal behavior is the most important characteristic of a useful objective. It identifies the kind of performance that will be accepted as proof that the learner has achieved the objective. The terminal behavior answers the question, "How do you know the learner has learned what you intended to teach?" But more importantly, it answers for the learner the question, "How will I know that I've learned what I'm supposed to learn?"

Here are three guidelines for using terminal behaviors:

1. Be detailed enough so that another competent person could recognize the target behavior.

2. Provide an assessment rubric and sample test items or evaluative tasks to specify the type of terminal behaviors the learner will be expected to perform.

3. Describe the situation in which the terminal behavior will be demonstrated.

The Criterion

The criterion in your learning objective provides the minimal acceptable performance level you expect of the learner — whether it's a skill, behavior, or cognitive activity. The criterion allows you to evaluate how well your students achieved the learning outcome. It also allows you to evaluate how effective your teaching was in helping students realize the objectives.

When writing the criterion you must be as specific as possible. The use of criterion and qualitative rubrics will help you in both creating a refined meaningful learning objective, and, in assessing student learning.

Your instructional objectives describe your educational intent from the standpoint of the learner. To describe the terminal behavior, (1) identify and name the behavior, (2) define the conditions under which the behavior will be applied, and (3) define the criterion of acceptable performance.

Write your objectives appropriate to the level to which you will apply them. The objectives for your course will likely be long-range and comprehensive (Example: "The student will be able to tell a story effectively using the four-stage narrative framework"), while the objectives for a single lesson in your course will be short range and specific (Example: "The student will be able to appropriately use one of three closure techniques to end a story presentation.").

Learning Objectives Checklist

Use the following checklist when writing your learning objectives:

☐ Is the learning objective written from the standpoint of the learner?

☐ Is the terminal behavior specified?

☐ Are the conditions under which the behavior should occur specified?

☐ Are the criteria of acceptable performance specified?

☐ Can someone else understand the full intent of the objective?

Getting Specific

While objectives need to be clear and specific in order to be effective, you don't need to be highly specific when writing your objectives. Below is an example of a learning objective from a religious studies course that has been written in general terms and then re-written several times, each one more specific:

1. Students will be able to read the Bible with understanding.

2. When given a Bible passage to read, the student will be able to answer questions about the content of the passage.

3. When given a Bible passage to read, the student will be able to identify the verses which identify the traits of the literary genre.

4. Students will be able to identify the passages which identify the literary traits specific to the Gospel of Matthew.

5. Students will be able to identify at least five passages from the Gospel of Matthew that illustrate the identity of the author.

6. Students will be able to recognize five passages cited in Handout 3 which illustrates the gospel author's Jewish identity.

Notice that the most useful instructional objectives in the above examples are those which fall somewhere in the middle of the continuum from very general to very specific. When learning objectives become too specific, they lose much of their value as a guide to study and become little more than test questions to be answered.

How to Craft Learning Objectives

Here are some ideas for crafting your learning objectives. As with any art form, instruction is a process, starting with crafting your objective. Brainstorm a bit: list the key principles, basic concepts, critical rules, and major big ideas that make up the content of your course or lesson. List as many as you can think of that fall within a reasonable range of difficulty for the level of learning you are striving for.

Define the cutoff point: given the amount of instructional time you have, how deeply can you reasonably go into the subject? How much coverage is reasonable or necessary to achieve the learning outcome? If you had time to teach only one critical point, what would it be?

How much can you assume about your students' familiarity with the material? What principles, concepts, procedures, and facts do you feel confident in assuming they already know? The answers to these pre-knowledge questions can define the starting point for the content you want to present. This point is important, because underestimating the appropriate starting point may bog the students down in material they already know. Overestimating how much your students know may result in confusion early on, and the need to "backtrack" and cover rudimentary or foundational knowledge.

Create Learning Outcomes for Deep Learning

Meaningful learning outcomes target deep learning. That is, they point to outcomes that go beyond rudimentary levels of learning. They aim to move the student to demonstrate deep understanding and complex cognitive application: comprehension, application, analysis, and other critical thinking behaviors.

One trap instructors fall into is too quickly adopting lover-level learning outcomes from a taxonomy, particularly, the popular Bloom's Taxonomy. For example, too many learning outcomes on even graduate level courses use "identify," "list," and "name" as the outcomes for learning. These are too simplistic and rudimentary to be meaningful, and, they do not provide sufficient evidence of deep learning. It is very possible for a student to satisfactory "list" or "identity" course or lesson content facts without actually comprehending or understanding them.

Along the same lines, too many learning outcomes use vague terms like "articulate," or "understand." Unless you provide a qualitative assessment rubric for particular learning activities or assessment products (a test, a project, a paper), terms like articulate and understand are meaningless. The questions you must answer for the learner is, "What does it mean to articulate?" "What does it mean to understand?"

When crafting your learning outcomes avoid using rudimentary levels of learning and vague descriptors of actions. Below are sample learning outcomes. See if you can discern how rudimentary outcomes will not lead to meaningful learning. See is you can discern the use of vague terms that make the outcome unclear:

At the conclusion of this session, the participant will be able to:

Demonstrate an understanding of the basic concept of quarkling by identifying three basic elements of the concept.

Articulate the difference between quarkling and the related concepts of quizpling and quipptain.

Explain the value of using quarkling as a foundational concept over other related concepts.

Name three examples of pastoral crisis intervention and site at least three biblical resources for pastoral care intervention.

Identify two principles of pastoral crisis intervention found in a case study.

Identify four of the six factors that are obstacles to therapeutic communication.

Apply Finklestein's principles of therapeutic communication in a role play situation.

Assess the effective use of therapeutic communication in a group therapy session.

Correctly identify five out of seven components of leadership through self-differentiation.

Correctly list five potential reactivity postures to self-differentiating leadership stances.

Given a case study, the student will predict how a self-differentiated leader would respond to statements of dissent.

Students should be able to interpret a Bible passage based on its literary genre.

Student should be able to list the five punctuation rules discussed in class.

The student should be able to label the major parts of an epistle.

Summary

Crafting effective learning objectives is a critical instructional skill. Like any skill, most beginning practitioners find it a challenge. It will not take long, however, to appreciate how developing and refining student learning objectives leads to more effective instruction. The learning objectives you craft will help you define the educational goals of your course, unit, or lesson. They will help you decide on the appropriate methods, learning experiences, and resources.

Writing and using learning objectives will make your course, or lesson, a much more effective learning experience for your students. For one thing, published learning objectives will demonstrate the effectiveness of your teaching, and, will make it easier to evaluate student learning. Taking the time to develop effective learning objectives makes it easier to design a more effective learning experience. Once you determine what you want your students to learn by the end of the course, you can make more informed choices about the scope of study (coverage). It will help you follow the educational adage, "Do not teach what you will not assess."

❖

Chapter 4

How to Begin Instruction

Sometime this week my wife and I will sit down in front of the television to watch a favorite T.V. program. As we settle down on the sofa with popcorn or chips and salsa a familiar splash screen reads "Law & Order," and we'll hear the familiar opening: "In the criminal justice system the people are represented by two separate but equally important parties: the police who investigate and the prosecutors who.... These are their stories." Followed by a dramatic "Boom-doom."

By now, regular viewers know what comes next:

Opening scene: two people walking down a dark and lonely NYC street, chatting about something interesting but inconsequential. One of them will see something that will make him or her cry out, "Oh, my God! Call 911." The other will rush over and see a body.

In the version we've liked best, detectives Lenny Briscoe and Ed Green (with his handy notepad and pencil) will show up at a secured scene, ask questions of the Medical Examiner, including asking about an estimated time of death. This opening sequence will end with Lenny making an insensitive but funny quip.

An initial investigation takes place, framed with quick, snappy dialogue between detectives Briscoe and Green and their commanding office, Lt. Anita Van Beuran. They'll interview people and bring in a couple of suspects for questing. At one point they'll have to backtrack because they discover they're going down the wrong track or they've been misled.

Eventually they make a dramatic arrest, and the scene shifts to the District Attorney's office where Assistant District Attorney Jack McCoy and Assistant District Attorney Serena Southerlyn put a case together (with Serena doing most of the legwork).

The episode moves on to the trial (after a failed attempt at negotiating a settlement). After much courtroom drama (much of it implausable), the jury gives its finding. Closing scene: the district attorneys share final thoughts as they walk toward the elevator at the end of the day.

Even the occasional television viewer is familiar with this opening format and plot element. Every successful TV series uses it. Actually there is really nothing new each week. The plot follows a familiar pattern—one which you could sketch out with little effort. What keeps us tuning in to our favorite, and predictable, shows each week is, in large part, the stimulation we experience in viewing the latest twist in chase scenes, shootouts, or lifesaving medical techniques. Once the show satisfies the viewer's appetite for thrills, excitement, or pathos, the story winds down, the heroes and heroines relax, the loose ends are all neatly tied together, and we can breathe easily once more, knowing that next week it will be back again.

It is no accident that TV uses this formula. Radio used it before TV, and before that dramatists practiced the art of teasing their audiences through a long list of weekly and monthly publications. Producers of popular television series meticulously plan, prepare, and direct their shows using techniques designed to get viewers "into" the show, to keep them glued to their sets, and to satisfy their needs for having participated in a complete experience.

Learning theorists as well as practitioners interested in teacher training have known for some time how effective these techniques can be when skillfully employed by teachers in a classroom setting. Educators have developed elaborate schemes for classifying and analyzing the techniques and their underlying concepts. Although research has identified 25 lesson presentation skills that are considered part of the classroom recitation process, the most frequently researched one has been introducing the lesson, or set induction.

The Functions of Set Induction

Set induction refers to those actions and statements by the teacher that are designed to relate the experiences of the students to the learning objectives of the lesson. By using set induction you put students in a receptive frame of mind that will facilitate learning. The instructional action of set induction serves several didactic functions during the course of the instructional process.

A. Starting Instruction

The first function of set induction is to focus student attention on the lesson. Simply put, set induction function alerts the student that the formal learning process has begin and it is time to "pay attention." The point to not miss here is that the student's brain needs this overt indicator in order to block out distraction and focus on the specific information-processing task related to instruction. They key to effective set induction is to make the start of instruction overt. Some teachers will ring a bell;

others train their classes to recognize a cue phrase ("Good morning, class" or, "Let's begin!"). However you choose to do it, your beginning set induction needs to be overt and clear.

One caution, however. Set inductions that alert the students that the learning process has started are very powerful. The brain believes it, and will focus with expectancy. The worst thing an instructor can do after this type of alert is to fail to begin instruction. To do so causes confusion in the learner. After hearing the alert induction for the start of instructional learning, the brain is "set" and expects to hear instruction. If instead the brain hears a rambling scattered dialogue about the weather, seating arrangements, non-academic questions ("Did everyone get a handout?"), or anything other than the start of instruction, it gets confused, becomes frustrated, and soon stops paying attention.

The longer you go on with non-instructional information after offering the set induction that announces the start of instruction, the more frustrated your students become, and, the more likely they'll tune out. I've seen instructors drone on for as long as 10 and 15 minutes after the "start" of the class. A quick scan of the body language in the classroom is evidence enough that most of the class members have stopped paying attention. This kind of teacher behavior is called a "false start." If you do this, you will need to "re-start" the instructional process by providing a new alert induction cue to the start of instruction. Failing to do so, the tendency is that you will move on with the instruction while most students are tuned out. That will cause the students to attempt to catch up at the point they re-engage: "Oh, have we started?" "Wait, what did I miss?"

B. Creating a Framework for Learning

The second function of set induction is to create an organizing framework for the ideas, principles, or information which is to follow. This is the same function that advanced organizers serve in the teaching-learning process. Using set induction as an advanced organizer does two important things for the leaner: (1) it helps the learner know what he or she will learn (answer the question, "What is this lesson about?"), and (2) it helps the learner know what to listen for and what to pay attention to. The learning principle behind this teacher instructional task is: if students are provide with a framework for what they are about to learn, then students will tend to focus better and learn more effective and efficiently. This is akin to the old adage in homiletics (preaching): "Tell them what you are going to tell them, tell them, then tell them what you told them."

C. Reinforcing Concepts Through Examples and Analogy

A third function of set induction is to extend the understanding and the application of abstract ideas (concepts) through the use of example or analogy. Concepts and principles that are presented abstractly can be difficult for students to comprehend. Additionally, even when a student grasps an abstract concept, it can be difficult for them to apply it to concrete, novel, or new situations. Using inductions that provide examples or analogies helps bridge abstract concepts to concrete application.

Abstract concepts are difficult attain, and, if they remain abstract and not anchored to a meaningful application in the life of the student, they tend to be forgotten. Remember, the brain's Job 1 is survival. If it does not see the meaningful application of an abstract concept, it will not expend the energy to retain it. Moving ideas, concepts and information from short-term memory to long-term memory takes energy and effort. Your students' brains need to believe that it's worth the effort! Using analogy inductions helps the student make a connection between the abstract and concrete experiences. This teacher behavior will often solicit early "Aha!" moments for students.

D. Curiosity, Interest, Motivation

Set induction can be used to elicit curiosity and interest in the lesson, and create motivation for the lesson. Tapping into curiosity and interest at the beginning of the lesson, through set induction, can help maintain attention throughout the lesson. Active student involvement at the begging of the learning experience increases students' interest in learning. Incorporate a learning activity that is closely related to the concept-attainment purpose of the lesson. For example, before a lesson on the concept of "categorization," the teacher may have groups categorize objects (role playing cards, baseball cards, a bag of leaves, the contents of their backpacks), a list (book titles, song titles, historical figures), or images (paintings, art objects, photographs). Give the students just a few minutes to categorize the items, then debrief by asking each group to provide a rationale for why they organized objects the way they did.

It is important, however, to differentiate between "interest," and "motivation." Making the learning experience interesting at the start of the lesson is important, and tickling curiosity helps the learning process. But interest has limited impact, it does not sustain a student's capacity to attain meaningful learning. Motivation, however, is a powerful force that leads to meaningful learning, especially for adult students. Motivation goes to need. What motivates a person to learn is a perceived or unrealized need. If at the beginning of the lesson you can demonstrate the need the students have for what is being taught, then students will more likely be motivated to learn in order to satisfy a need. That motivation will more likely be sustained over time than merely making the lesson "interesting" at the start of the lesson.

The most effective and powerful set induction activities are those that identify for the student a perceived or unrealized need. Once the need is identified, explain how the topic, concept, or skill the student will learn will satisfy that need.

Examples of When to Use Set Induction

The list of examples below illustrates the many ways set induction can help the teaching-learning process. The common function that runs through these examples is the teacher's act in shifting focus and making transitions in the learning process overt.

To begin a long unit of work in which the class will study a new topic or subject.

To introduce a new concept or principle.

To initiate a discussion.

To begin a skill-building activity.

To introduce a film, video clip, or sound recording.

To initiate a question-and-answer session.

To present a guest speaker.

To introduce a homework assignment.

To begin a laboratory exercise.

To identify for the student how the lesson will help meet a perceived or unrealized need.

Summary

In this chapter we reviewed the instructional skill of set induction. This skill provides powerful pedagogical means for starting the learning experience in ways that help students gain motivation for learning and focus attention. While primarily used for marking the beginning of instruction, induction serves pedagogical functions throughout the arc of an instructional set, like introducing learning segments or activities. In the next chapter we will review how induction can be used to move the flow of instruction and facilitate learning in the student.

❖

Chapter 5

Using Induction to Carry the Lesson

The single greatest impediment to learning in the instructional context is confusion. The student cannot learn what he or she does not understand. Effective instructors know how to teach in ways that keep the students engaged, give clear direction, avoid confusion, and assess the level of comprehension during the learning process. When students are confused by poor directions, or, scattered dialogue, tangential information, and poor transitions, they "get lost" in the disrupted flow of learning. When this happens, students tend to stop paying attention, and, learning ceases to happen.

Effective teachers avoid confusion by using the powerful instructional technique of induction. In the last chapter we reviewed one type of instruction to start the instructional experience.

Set induction refers to instructional actions taken by a teacher to begin a lesson or other classroom activity. A set induction can introduce a topic and get students focused and interested in the day's lesson. It gets students' attention and puts them in the right frame of mind to learn. Set induction can also orient the student to the teaching and learning processes they will experience. In this chapter, we will learn three specific types of induction.

The Three Types of Inductions

During the course of instruction you can use three types of induction sets. Each is applicable during certain phases of the instructional arch (beginning, middle, and end). The three types of induction sets are orientation, transition, and evaluation.

ORIENTATION SET

In the last chapter you were introduced to the first function of induction, the orientation set. You will use an orientation induction set to gain the students' attention at the beginning of the instruction, and to focus their attention on the presentation you are about to begin. This is the important action that "cues" the students that the lesson is about to begin and what it is they will be studying.

For the orientation induction set you can build on the student's prior knowledge of experience by using an activity, event, object, illustration, or person which you know students have interest in or experience with. This powerful cue provides a structure or framework which helps your students visualize the content or activities of the presentation to come. This action applies the fundamental principle of building new learning on the student's prior learning. Or, as I put it, "Never invite the learner into a vacuum."

To use an orientation set:

Use it at the beginning of the lesson or the beginning of a course, or lesson

Use it to "set" the students' focus and attention on the concept you are about to introduce

Use an event, experience, or activity familiar to your students and in which they have some interest.

Explain how the orientation set provides a frame of reference for what the students are about to learn.

TRANSITION SET

The second type of induction is the transition set. You will use this action to provide a smooth transition from known or already covered material to new or unknown material. To use this induction set you will depend heavily on examples (either verbal or nonverbal), analogies, and student activities you know students have interest in or experience with.

Transition induction sets help students know where they are in the arch of the learning experience. If you fail to provide overt cues in the instructional transition you risk losing students along the way. Transition set cues may be as simple as a verbal cue of, "Let's review what we have just learned before applying it in an experiment." Or, "We've just learned that. . . . Now, let's see how this can apply to. . . ."

To use a transition set,

Provide a smooth transition from what the students already know (facts, experiences, concepts) to the new material to be covered in the lesson

Use a learning activity which is familiar to the students, and which can provide a bridge to the next part of the lesson

Use the activity to explain or introduce the connection with the next part of the learning process or the new knowledge to be acquired.

EVALUATION SET

The third type of induction is the evaluation set. You will use this instructional behavior to test for student comprehension of the concepts you have been teaching before moving on to new material, a skill-building activity, or an application activity. This induction action uses student-centered activities or student-developed examples and analogies that will provide you with evidence of understanding the instructional content.

This evaluation set will also help you uncover misunderstandings your students may have and will allow you to provide correctives before moving ahead with the learning experience and instructional arch. Remember that the greatest obstacle to learning in the instructional setting is confusion. If you do not test for comprehension before moving on to the next part of the lesson's concepts-acquisition stage students will become confused. It is more effective to test for comprehension and ensure all students understand before moving forward than to stumble into confusion from misunderstandings later in the lesson and have to pause to review, re-explain, and clarify.

To use the evaluation set,

Briefly summarize what students have learned so far

Initiate a discussion or question-and-answer segment

During the discussion or question-and-answer review assess how well students understand the concepts of the lesson

Solicit student-developed examples to demonstrate how well students understand the concept

Provide correctives to misunderstandings. Explain why a student response is incorrect, incomplete, naïve, insufficient, or inadequate

Provide reinforcement to correct responses and evidence of learning. Explain why a student response is correct, accurate, appropriately illustrative, or adequate.

Summary

Set induction refers to instructional actions to begin a lesson or other classroom activity that help the teaching-learning process. A set induction can serve a variety of important pedagogical functions, from introducing a topic, getting students focused and interested in the day's lesson, and incorporating an advanced organizer. Induction gets students' attention and puts them in the right frame of mind to learn. Set induction can also orient the student to the teaching and learning processes they will experience. In this chapter, we reviewed three specific types of induction you can use throughout the arc of instruction: orientation, transition, and evaluation. Mastering the skill of using induction sets will help you keep students engaged and avoid confusion. The use of induction sets is one way you can control the discourse and flow of instruction.

❖

Chapter 6

How To Ask Effective Questions

If there is one instructional skill that can be called "the single most important teaching skill" out of the nine essential instructional skills it is the skill of how to ask a question. When asking questions in the instructional setting a good teacher must pay attention to not only what kinds of questions to ask (the category of question and the type of question), but, must also be intentional about how to ask questions.

Asking the Right Kinds of Questions

Questions can serve different functions in teaching. Questions serve a variety of functions in the instructional act, and can fall under two categories: instructional questions (those having directly to do with learning and concepts-acquisition), and non-instructional questions (e.g., procedural, classroom management, etc.). Here are examples for each category:

Instructional questions

- Gain information from students to diagnose their understanding and evaluate their performance

- Lead students to consider new ideas and make use of ideas already learned

- Assess the knowledge students bring to the class so lessons can be made to meet their needs

- Help students clarify their ideas and thought processes

- Encourage students to ask their own questions

- Provide a means for stimulating class discussion

- Challenge beliefs and guide reconsideration of values students hold

- Revise information from a previous session

- Provide a springboard for discussion.

Non-Instructional Questions

- Identify students' interests and backgrounds

- Provide motivation by encouraging students to actively participate in learning

- To assess the effectiveness of your own teaching

- Develop rapport with students

- Get a student having difficulties back on task.

- To check on progress on a learning activity

- To check on the state of comfort in the room

- To inquire about students' emotional states

- To ask administrative questions.

While both categories of questions are legitimate in the instructional setting, the most effective questions to ask in order to promote learning and concept-acquisition are instructional questions. Instructional questions are those which are directly related to the content of study, the concept under consideration, or which are directly related to the learning outcome. Spending too much class time on non-instructional questions not only eats up valuable instructional time, but it also deadens your students' ability to "hear" good questions when you ask them.

Try to minimize the number of non-instructional questions you ask. For instance, minimize the number of procedural questions you ask ("Is everybody ready?" "Are we ready to begin?" "Are we ready to move on with the lesson?" "Where's the signup sheet now? Are we passing it around?"). Minimize the number of administrative questions you ask ("Is everyone on the right page in the textbook?" "Did everybody sign in?" "Are there enough handouts for everyone?"). Minimize the number of classroom management questions you ask ("Is everyone ready to line up?" "Who's talking?" "Do we have enough chairs for everyone?" "Can we make a circle with the chairs, please?") Do not ask about the obvious. If something is self-evident don't waste time by asking about it. Be sure your question helps lead your students toward the learning outcome and concept-acquisition you are after.

The Correct Way To Ask A Question

Here is what you need to know about asking questions in the instructional setting: there is a way to ask a question that facilitates the learning process; asking questions any other way will inhibit the learning process in the group. To put it another way, it matters how you ask questions in the instructional setting. If you ask a question one certain way it helps students learn, but if you ask it any other way it actually inhibits learning.

The one way to ask a question in the instructional setting is a four-step technique. to use when asking a question in the instructional setting is as follows:

1. Ask the question.

    a. Ask only one question at a time.

    b. Do not repeat the question.

2. Pause and wait for a response from the learner.

3. Acknowledge the response.

4. Ask the next question.

Regardless of what level of learning question you ask, or what type of question you ask, you must always use the same four-step technique when asking a question.

Ask Only One Question at a Time

Step one in the correct way to ask a question in the instructional setting is to ask only one question at a time. If you do not do step one (ask only one question at a time) you risk subjecting your learners to "question overload." Question overload happens when you ask two or more questions back to back without an intervening student response. Repeating a question without an intervening student response is another form of question overload. The problem with question overload is that it confuses the learner, and when learners are confused they stop thinking (because the brain stops paying attention) and therefore stop learning.

> **Question Overload Occurs When You**
> • Ask two questions back to back without an intervening student response
> • Repeat a question without an intervening student response.

Pause and Wait For A Student Response

The second step in asking questions correctly is to pause and wait for a student response. If you do not do step two (pause and wait for a student response) then you set your students up for a couple of unfortunate consequences. First, if you do not pause for a learner to respond to your question you'll probably wind up answering your own question, or asking another question (and thereby engaging in question overload). If you answer your own question as a course of habit you essentially train your students that when you, the teacher, ask a question in class it is not a "real" question. They learn that you really don't expect them to answer the question, because you answer your own questions! Therefore, they don't have to think about the questions you ask in class. I'm often asked how long an instructor should wait for a response after asking a question. My answer is, "As long as it takes." Silence allows students time to think about the question and about how to construct their response. The more time you give students to think the better their answers will tend to be. Responses that are fast are not necessarily the best, and often are offered by eager or extraverted students who go with what they believe is the "right answer." Avoid creating an environment where the fastest student always gets to answer first.

The most challenging aspect of step two seems to be that most teachers are afraid of silence. They assume that silence after a question they've asked means that nothing is happening. In fact, however, if the teacher has asked a good question, then silence is probably an indicator that something good is happening: the students are thinking about the question and their response to it. If you have a tendency to answer your own question because you are afraid of silence, then the trick is to (1) reframe your understanding of what that silence means, and (2) raise your tolerance level for silence above that of your group's tolerance level for silence.

Remember that if you are just beginning to implement this essential instructional skill one thing you may need to do is to re-train your class members that when you ask a question it's a real question and you expect them to think about it and respond.

Acknowledge the Response

Step three in asking questions in the instructional setting is to overtly and verbally acknowledge the student response. Ignoring step three inhibits learning in two ways. First, you in effect, ignore the learner who has taken the time to think about your question and has formulated a response to it. Second, you do not clue in the respondent, or the rest of the class, as to whether that response was right or wrong, complete or incomplete, acceptable or not. Remember that you are teaching a group of learners, and as such, your teaching actions must help the group as a whole learn together. When you acknowledge a student response you let the learner know the quality of his or her response, and you help the rest of the class members stay with the dialogue by not leaving them behind or confused.

Beginning teachers sometimes are afraid of what to do when a student answers a question "wrong," or gives a confusing response. I think the first thing to remember is that a good question does not solicit a "right" or "wrong" response. This means that an effective instructor works hard at learning how to ask good questions—precise, specific, and interesting. Second, it is more favorable to get a "wrong" answer than no answer! For one thing, a student who gives a wrong answer is at least engaged and putting forth effort! For another, a wrong response can alert the instructor to misunderstandings or can be a way to test for comprehension. If one student gives evidence of a lack of comprehension through a "wrong answer," the chances are that there are also others in the room that haven't arrived at an accurate understanding yet. A good instructor can handle a wrong answer to keep learning going. "Wrong" or incomplete answers are helpful because they can help the teacher assess the class' level of comprehension. Upon hearing a wrong answer the teacher may think, "O.k., sounds like we're not there yet," and can then continue the instructional process—through explication, discourse, or question-and-answer dialogue—to lead the class toward the goal of concept-attainment.

Here are additional guidelines for asking effective questions:

Be Clear. Avoid vagueness terms ("might," "may," "perhaps," "some people," "sometimes," "could be," "at times," "maybe," "often," "actually," etc.). Be precise when asking questions; say what you mean and mean what you say. Vagueness terms make for poor questions because they lack sufficient specificity so as to cause confusion in the mind of the learner.

Focus on ONE idea or thought. Each question you ask should be about one thing and only one thing. Keep your question structure simple.

Ask More Open-ended Questions. Avoid simplistic questions that can be answered with a yes or a no or an "I don't know." Good questions are interesting. They solicit exploration and imaginative responses. Good questions encourage students to paraphrase, interpret, offer opinion, speculate, offer a hunch, or explicate.

Make Your Questions Interesting. The most interesting questions are those that are more complex, that challenge our assumptions and that tap into our imagination. Ask more questions that have divergent responses (many correct answers or even unknown answers) as well as convergent questions (which yield single or limited number of answers). Try starting some of your questions in these ways:

- Why do you think…?

- What if…?

- If today…?

- If you could…what…?

- What might…?

- How would you reply to…?

- Pretend you know…tell me…? (for when you get that learner who responds to a question with "I don't know.").

Summary

Asking effective instructional questions is the single most important skills every teacher must master. In the instructional setting there is only one way to ask a question that promotes learning and avoids inhibiting learning. Applying this four-step technique to asking a question in the instructional context will immediately make you a more effective instructor. The biggest challenge will be to practice the skill until it becomes second nature to you. The second challenge will be to re-train your class on the instructional function of questions if you have trained them poorly by using an ineffective questioning technique.

Chapter 7

How To Respond to Student Responses

In the last chapter we reviewed the single most important teaching skill: asking effective instructional questions. Using the four step technique presented in that chapter will enhance learning in the classroom while avoiding impediments to learning, like imposing question overload. To review, here is the four-step technique for asking questions in the instructional setting:

1. Ask the question.
   a. Ask only one question at a time.
   b. Do not repeat the question.
2. Pause and wait for a response from the learner.
3. Acknowledge the response.
4. Ask the next question.

In this chapter we will go into more details about steps 2 to 4: how to handle student responses so as to continue the process of learning. Below is a repertoire of techniques for responding to and using student responses in the process of learning. The purpose of using these techniques is to foster critical thinking and meaningful learning on the part of the student. As you will see, the responses are intended to push the learning process back to the students. These techniques follow the adage "students are the agents of learning, not the teacher." While instruction is highly dependent on the teacher's application of instructional behaviors, the learning process must be directed toward the student's experience of the learning process. Use the techniques below when managing students' responses to move the learning process.

Using the four step questioning technique will facilitate instructional dialogue and interactive learning. Step 3 is critically important in that it helps avoid confusion, provides over cues for comprehension, and helps keep the instructional dialogue moving. In the instructional context the teacher's acknowledgement of the students' response must be overt and clear. It is insufficient to merely nod one's head as an acknowledgement. Doing so does not provide a clear enough indication about the quality of a response and leaves the student, and the class, confused about whether the answer was right, wrong, incomplete, true or false.

Acknowledge student responses verbally, even if it's merely a "thank you," before asking the next question (step 4). An acknowledgement of a student response becomes more effective, however, when it provides conditional cues as to the quality of the response: "Yes, that's correct." "Thank you, good try, but that's not correct." "Good, answer, but there's more to the question."

Redirect to Student Dialogue

One way to respond to a student response that helps keep the learning focused on the student learning experience is to ask students to comment on a student's response rather than responding immediately yourself. Acknowledge the student response (a simple, "Thank you," will suffice), and follow up by asking other class members, "Can anyone add more to that?"

"Would you say it different?" "Was there anything missing from that response?" "What else can we say about that?" "How would you answer the question differently?"

Redirecting the question to the class in general (by asking for an answer or comment, or for an elaboration upon the issue), not only encourages more student participation, but it also demonstrates that peers are a resource for learning.

Lead Students to Dig Deeper

Sometimes students' answers to your question will not be fully formed. A "first response" to a question is helpful to getting the dialogue going, but often these are not well-thought out answers reflective of deep thinking. Help students dig deeper by asking them to clarify their responses. Ask them to define vague terms, or to rephrase their response. Help them to develop their response rather than filling in the gaps for them. Ask, 'tell me more about that' 'what do you mean by. . . ,' 'why do you think that . . . ,' 'could you clarify that further . . . ,' 'please repeat' 'I don't understand what you mean by . . . .' When a student uses a technical or a vague term, acknowledge the response and ask, "What do you mean by that term?"

Challenge Uncritical Assumptions

Helping students become aware of unexamined assumptions leads to critical thinking and self-awareness. Challenging students' uncritical assumptions is especially helpful in helping them understand how they are thinking — or not. Help your students uncover their ways of thinking, how they progressed and how they arrived at their conclusion.

Acknowledge the student response, then, ask, "How did you come to that conclusion?" "How do you know that to be true?"

When challenging assumptions you are not asking a student to justify a belief or defend whether or not they believe that what they believe is the truth. What you are encouraging the student to do is to articulate a rationale for why they believe what they believe is true. Let your students know that what you are doing is simply asking them to supply sound and valid reasons to show that what they are claiming to be true is in fact true, or worthy of belief.

Uncover Appeals to Authority

It has been estimated that in most college classes, at least 30% of what students repeat is actually the opinion of the professor, and not necessarily based on any direct evidence. Similarly, in religious education contexts, the majority of opinions and beliefs are based on authority figures, rather than the result of critical examination. This is a major impediment in a movement from received faith to owned faith—which is an important step toward faith maturity. In all contexts, it is the danger of remaining in naïve thinking and failing to exercise critical thinking.

Effective instructors watch for appeals to authority in student responses that negate critical thinking. During the instructional dialogue listen to student responses and challenge uncritical and unexamined reliance on authority that shortcut critical thinking on the part of the students. To challenge uncritical authority-based answers, ask, "Where do you get the information to support what you are saying?" "Where did you get your information?" "Why do you believe your source?" "Is that really your opinion, or is it someone else's?"

Foster Alternative Thinking

One of the greatest impediments to learning, and to critical thinking, is bias. Bias leaves us blind to alternative thinking. While it is a challenge to consider that our thinking, beliefs, and interpretations of the facts may be wrong, it is a necessary skill for fostering creativity and for problem-solving.

Students, as do most people, will tend to hold one position very strongly, against all others. In the course of the learning process students may assert, either implicitly or explicitly, that what they believe to be true must be objective truth. This leaves little room to consider different viewpoints, and leaves little capacity to listen to the merit of alternate perspectives. When replying to student responses that demonstrate bias, challenge them to explain clearly, and fairly, opposing viewpoints, along with good evidence if appropriate, and explain why they disagree. You may ask, "What if you are wrong in what you believe?" "Can you offer two sources that disagree with you and explain why?" "What other perspectives on that may there be, and can they have a valid point?" "Can you give me an alternate explanation for this phenomenon?"

How to Handle Wrong Student Responses

Often teachers and students are concerned about avoiding wrong answers from students. So much so that many students learn to not risk responding to a question lest they not provide the "right" answer. But in the teaching-learning process of instruction, a wrong answer is better than no answer. For one thing, a wrong student response is a helpful cue to the instructor that "we're not there yet." Either students have not acquired basic comprehension, or, they are still working on a misunderstanding.

A wrong answer may help the instructor realize that his or her explanations, explications, or instructional presentation has not been effective.

Student responses that are "wrong" often are merely incomplete. In that case, overtly and clearly assert what is "right" with the response, but identify that it is incomplete. You can provide the incomplete part, ask the student to try again, or, redirect to the class to build on the student's response and provide the missing component.

In all cases of wrong answers in the instructional process, it is important to provide overt cues as to the student's response. Never ignore a wrong answer. Provide an overt and verbal cue about whether an answer is correct or incorrect. Remember that instruction is directed at the whole class. Students need overt indications about whether or not another student's response was correct, incorrect, or incomplete. Realize that when you asked the question and one student responded, others in the class formulated a response in their minds and are comparing their unspoken answer with the student's answer.

There are several ways to respond to a student's wrong answer that do not interrupt the instructional flow and learning process. Here are some examples:

"Good try, but no, that's not correct."

"That's partially correct. What else do you need to add to that response?"

"Thank you. Explain a little more, I think you are correct, but it's not clear."

"Unpack that a bit more so I'm sure I understand what you are saying."

"I'm not sure you are using some terms correctly. Can you define the terms you are using, or say it in a different way?"

Summary

The give and take of instructional learning requires the teacher to be adept at asking questions and handing student responses in a way that move the learning process forward. In this chapter we reviewed the correct technique for asking a question in the instructional setting, and, how to handle student responses. Mastering these instructional skills will allow you to teach in a way that facilitates deep learning by your students.

Engaging students by using question-and-answer dialogical learning makes for a dynamic and interactive teaching-learning experience that makes the classroom instruction experience interesting and meaningful. It allows the teacher to effectively develop the acquisition of concepts and principles from rudimentary to more in-depth and nuanced understanding

❖

Chapter 8

How to Maintain Attention

Here is a fundamental pedagogical truth: students learn what they pay attention to. That may seem obvious, but it is often overlooked in the instructional process. A significant part of the instructor's role is to facilitate that to which the students need to pay attention in order to learn. Because of the countless stimuli and distractions vying for students' attention during the course of a lesson or learning experience, they need help to know what to focus on.

Fortunately, there are several specific instructional techniques teachers can use to focus students on the learning process, and, to maintain attention throughout the instructional lesson. Additionally, understanding how the brain achieves attentional states can help the instructor know how to keep and hold students' attention during the learning process.

The Brain and Attention

One of the ways to capture and maintain students' attention is to tap into one of the key characteristics of the brain's cortex, its ability to detect and create patterns of meaning. The most important concept related to students' attentional states is this: students pay attention to what they understand, and cease to give attention to what confuses them. This process involves deciphering visual and auditory cues, recognizing relationships, and indexing information.

The brain's capacity to interpret and create patterns of meaning is the key to gaining the brain's attention. Recognizing patterns depends heavily on the prior experience a student brings to learning experience. Our neural patterns are continually revised as new experiences provide us with additional information, insights, and corrections. In fact, we can think of learning as the extraction of meaningful patterns from what seems random and disconnected, in other words, making sense of what does not make sense.

Here is the important point: a student never really cognitively understands something until they can either (1) fit it into an existing cognitive model or schema, or (2) create a new model or metaphor that is derived from their unique personal experience of the world.

Students' comprehension increases when they are able to create a mental model for the material they are trying to learn. However, this does not often happen without intervention from the instructor. Students do not always know what to pay attention to and may need overt cues as to the meaning of what they are focusing on. Therefore, instructors need to apply those teacher actions that demonstrate to students what to pay attention to, why it is important, and how it connects to prior learning and to new knowledge.

Generally speaking, learning results from the neural linkages between new experiences with cognitive maps and value centers (including emotional states—what we feel strongly about, and beliefs in which we have made an emotional investment because they help us make meaning). In other words, we are learning when we can relate the knowledge from one area to another and then make it personal and relevant. Just because a teacher says something is important does not automatically mean the student will believe it. Unless the student can immediately see its connection to prior learning (knowledge, assumptions, and beliefs) new information may remain meaningless.

How to Hook the Brain's Attention

The level of attention your students are able to apply to a learning situation is limited by their perception of its value. Remember that the brain is most alert to information that helps ensure its survival. This is the state that elicits attention: the perception that what is being learned is related to one's survival—physical or existential, immediate or consequentially. Consider, for example, how your brain kicks into action when viewing a commercial that is advertising something you need versus something you don't.

The brain is miserly with the energy it expends on things not related to its survival, so it does not attend to all of the data from stimuli that surrounds it. It sorts out that which is less critical to its survival, or, which is confusing and not related to what it is immediately giving attention to. Understanding that the brain has a built-in bias for certain types of stimuli, we can create the environment and experiences that will help the learners focus on aspects of learning that are personally meaningful to them. A natural prioritizing process is occurring all the time in our students, consciously and unconsciously. To the brain, contrast and emotion win hands down, with novelty being a strong third.

Any stimuli you introduce in the classroom which is either novel or provides a strong emotional response, will immediately gain your students' attention. However, you should strive to differentiate between a student need and an interest. A perceived need will solicit deeper attention than something that is merely interesting. Remember, meaningful information is retained, while information that is perceived as insignificant is forgotten. This is the reason students ask, "Will this be on the test?" If the answer is "Yes, this will be on the test," the student sees the information necessary for existential survival (to pass the course). If the answer is "No," then no matter how interesting, or important, the information is, the student will not make the effort to pay attention or retain it.

Teachers complain often that learners today are often on stimuli overload—by television media, smart phones, tablets, etc. Consequently, in the relatively sedate learning environment of a classroom they may feel bored, listless, and detached. Teachers who know how to capitalize on the brain's attentional biases, however, can get and keep their students' attention longer. This is only half the battle, however. The other half is learning how to engage students in meaningful learning so that the learner begins to drive their own attention and learning process. In this sense, the teacher becomes less of the "show," and the learners themselves, become the directors of their learning.

Strategies to Get and Maintain Attention

- Use advanced organizers that provide three things: (1) introduce novelty, (2) connect to prior learning or experiences, and (2) relate to meaning in the student's life (address a student's need).

- Provide a learning process that gives learners more control and accountability.

- Engage students in creating classroom rituals, projects, rules, procedures, and consequences.

- Provide students with choices in the course of study and ensure their learning environment reflects a sense of freedom, individual expression, and choice.

- Encourage students to pursue interesting life-like projects that will engage their curiosity and natural passions.

- Acknowledge individual learning differences and diverse lifestyles.

- Capitalize on the brain's bias for high contrast, visually and metaphorically.

- Encourage collaborative learning through projects or group work.

What Influences Attention

We know that attention level is determined by the interaction of various factors, such as: 1) the particular sensory input (i.e., a page in a textbook, a video, the teacher's voice); 2) the data's intensity or perceived importance (i.e., novelty, threat, opportunity, or pain); and 3) the brain's chemical "flavor of the moment" (i.e., hormone, peptide, and neurotransmitter levels).

The sequence of elements in the attentional process are:

1) initial alarm or notice (i.e., "Hey, something's happening here");

2) orientation (i.e., "Where do I focus?");

3) identification (i.e., "What is it?"); and

4) decision (i.e.. "This is what I need to do with this information.").

The answer to the "what" question (number 3 above) will determine how much and how long attention a student will focus on the stimulus. If we were to use imaging devices to observe what happens in the brain at various attention levels, we would a see a greater flow of energy to specific areas when the subject is at a high attention level. In short, when one's attention level is up, we can observe specialized brain activity that indicates an increase in attention level.

So, how does a student's brain know what to pay attention to in the moment? The secret is that the visual system (which is responsible for about 80 to 90 percent of incoming information in non-impaired learners) is not a one-way street. Information flows both ways, back and forth, from our eyes to the thalamus, to the visual cortex, and back again. This feedback is the mechanism which "shapes" a student's attention so that they can focus on one particular thing, like a teacher's lecture, a visual stimulus, or page on a book. Amazingly, the "attention headquarters" in the brain gets feedback from the cortex at nearly six times the amount that originates from the retina. Somehow, the brain corrects incoming images to help students stay attentive. But once it has reached its capacity, which is very low, it filters out incoming stimuli. In other words, the brain has an intrinsic mechanism for limiting the input it receives.

We absorb so much information that downtime is necessary to process it all. If it seems that your students have "stopped paying attention," consider that they may be doing something important to their learning process—reflecting. Down time, in fact, is absolutely necessary for learners to make sense of the information by integration with existing knowledge and by confirming that is has personal meaning. The amount of information an individual can take in before they reach a saturation point varies from person to person, but every learner eventually must go into reflection mode if new learning is to become absorbed by moving from short term memory to long term memory. In our role as educators, we can offset problems by paying more attention to this basic need. Plan reflective activities after each new learning session. Sometimes just a change in stimuli or context can allow the learner's brain to process new information and turn them into insights: a walk, a music session, a stretching session, or a taking a few minutes to make a visual mind-map.

Fostering Meaning-Making in Instruction

Humans are natural meaning-seeking and meaning-making organisms. But while the impulse and need to search for meaning is innate, the outcome of that effort is not automatic. Since meaning is internally oriented, highly personal and subjective, excessive input can conflict with the process of meaning-making. An important principle to remember is that you can either have your learner's attention or they can be about the work of making meaning, but never both at the same time. Reflective learning is the key to helping students make meaning of what they are learning.

One powerful method for helping students make meaning is to use small group discussion after new concepts or information is introduced during a period of direct instruction. This allows students to interpret the information and generate questions relevant to their personal experiences and contexts. Reflective assignments can include examples, case study scenarios, "what if" scenarios, and questions or prompts that encourage learners to find personal meaning in the new concepts or information learned.

During reflection experiences the brain filters new information through prior learning, experiences, and assumptions. It looks for links, associations, past experiences and procedural thinking as it seeks to make learning meaningful. This association and integrating process can only occur during reflective experience. Design your lessons to include some kind of reflection time (e.g., writing in journals or small group discussion) to help the brain do its meaning-making work after presenting new material. Remember that the more complex the concepts or information you present to students, the more reflection time they'll need.

Using Stimulus Variation to Gain Attention

Stimulus variation refers to those teacher actions designed to maintain student attention during the course of a lesson by varying the presentation stimuli. Master instructors know how and when to use the rich repertoire of stimulus variation during an instructional set during a lesson presentation.

The repertoire of stimulus variation consists of movements, sounds, or visual impressions which change or vary, with intention, during the learning experience. Your students can watch or listen to the same sight or sound only so long before they need a change in stimuli. This is more than a matter of a "short attention span" syndrome. TV and film directors understand this challenge well. Once they have gained the viewer's attention, they must hold it. They hold the viewer's attention by shifting the pace of dialogue, changing the music, shifting the viewing angle, shifting from dialogue to action, use fade-ins and fade-outs, shift from one locale to another, and use numerous other audio and visual techniques to make certain the audience stays engaged.

In the instructional context, the teacher needs to be attentive to the ways he or she is both a source of, and an orchestrator of stimuli. Awareness of this dynamic is important because stimulus variation can be a help or a hindrance to learning. The better an instructor becomes at understanding, applying, and controlling stimulus variation during the course of the teaching-learning process, the more effective she or he will be in attaining and maintaining students' attention. Additionally, by skillfully applying stimulus variation techniques, teachers can reduce the level of interference, or "noise," a student's brain must filter out in order to pay attention and understand.

Consider, for a moment, the kinds of interference or "noise" you, the teacher, must overcome in the average classroom situation. You can easily identify several, but here are four particular categories that contain the most challenging interferences.

1. Getting off-point. This kind of "noise" occurs when the instructor provides non-instructional information, engages in scattered dialogue, or uses excessive talk. For example, when the instructor chases rabbits, launches into asides, and provides information that is not directly related to the goal of the instruction set, mainly, helping the learner acquire understanding of the concept under study. When instructors get "off point" it confuses the learners, and confusion is the jumping off point for

ceasing to pay attention. Students do not pay attention to what confuses them.

2. Tuning out on the part of the learner. While you can work on becoming more effective in avoiding getting off point, this second challenge to maintaining student attention is more difficult to manage. Given the "noise" and distractions inherent in a learning setting, and given the limited amount of information students are able to take in at any given moment, "tuning out" is inevitable. Tuning out on the part of a learner can be due to many factors, like a lack of interest in the subject matter, learning disabilities, concerns over personal problems, or daydreaming. Each of these conditions internal to the student can be a strong deterrent to maintaining attention. Effective instructors know how to watch for cues that students are "tuning out" and employ stimulus variation to help them re-focus without causing a disruption in the flow of instruction, or causing anxiety.

3. An uncomfortable or distracting environment. Physically uncomfortable surroundings are another source of distraction from learning. Overheated or overly-cooled rooms take a toll on students' attention span and focus as the brain shifts its focus from learning to physical discomfort. Excessive noise levels from open rooms can make it difficult for teachers to maintain attention during a lesson. Even aesthetically unpleasant classrooms (clutter, too much furniture, unclean, crowded) may have a detrimental effect on the student's ability to pay attention.

4. Semantic confusion. This teacher behavior happens when the instructor's communication leads to confusion on the part of learners, and therefore causes them to stop paying attention. Semantic confusion can happen when a teacher over-explains something, or gives unclear or convoluted directions.

Semantic confusion often occurs when the instructor assumes prior knowledge or experience on the part of the learner and therefore proceeds with instruction without background, context, or point of reference. Students feel like they came in at the middle of a story, get confused, and stop paying attention.

Effective teachers monitor how these actions negatively impact instruction problems and work to avoid them by using stimulus variation techniques. The skillful use of these techniques will enable the teacher to (1) focus and maintain student attention on the lesson, (2) help students "track" the flow of instruction, and (3) change the pace of the lesson in order to maintain attention.

Stimulus Variation Categories

Below are five categories of stimulus variation that are part of the repertoire of every excellent instructor. The categories are: kinesic variation, focusing, shifting interaction, pausing, shifting senses.

1. Kinesic Variation

Kinesic variation is when an instructor physically moves from one location, or space, to another in the classroom for the purpose of maintaining student attention, emphasizing transition, or otherwise helping students maintain focus on the instruction. In this variation technique, a teacher may (a) move from one side to the other at the front of the classroom, (b) move from front to back and then from back to front, (c) move among, in front or, or behind students.

In this technique, the teacher's physical shift from one part of the room to the other causes the students' attention to be focused directly on the teacher during the presentation. This technique takes advantage of one of the brain's fundamental alert systems: watching for movement. These movements, however, should be natural and congruent with the message and movement of the teacher's verbal instruction. Rapid, jerky, or nervous movements can distract students, interrupting learning by causing confusion.

2. Focusing

Focusing is the instructor's way of intentionally controlling the direction of student attention. This action is accomplished either through verbal statements, through specific gestures or by a combination of the two. Here is a list of examples of the focusing stimulus variation in three categories, verbal, gesture, and a combination of the two.

Verbal Marker Expressions

- "Look at that diagram!"

- "Listen closely to this!"

- "Here's something really important!"

- "Watch what happens when I connect these two points!"

- "Examine the diagram carefully!"

- "Observe the difference in the colors!"

- "See the picture?"

Gestural

- Using a pointer to indicate an object you want the students to focus on.

- Turning your body in the direction of an object.

- Nodding your head for positive reinforcement.

- Using your hands expressively.

- Motioning with your arms.

- Raising your eyebrows.

- Smiling.

- Frowning.

Verbal-Gestural

- You point to diagram and say, "Look at that diagram!"

- You nod in direction from which sound is to come and say, "Listen closely to this!"

- You tap on the blackboard where you have written a statement, or, drawn a diagram, and say, "Here's something really important!"

- You use a laser pointer on a slide and say, "Follow this diagram carefully!"

3. Shifting Interaction

In the classroom setting there are three primary ways an instructor can shift interaction. There are: teacher-to-class, teacher-to-student, student-to-student, student-to-teacher. Teacher-to-class interaction is the default teacher-centered instructional style where the teacher is usually lecturing or demonstrating to the class as a whole. Although questions may be asked, they are directed to the group as a whole rather than to a specific individual. For the majority of time during an instructional set, this is the default interaction. Maintaining a high level of attention in this is very difficult, as it requires the instructor to hold the attention of every student in the group at the same time, at the same level of engagement, over time.

You can continue an instruction set and maintain attention by shifting to a teacher-student interaction. This is a teacher-directed rather than teacher-centered instructional style, but it shifts the flow of communication to student recitation and/or discussion. You may use instructional questions to engage an individual student in the lesson while maintaining the attention of the entire class. One must be careful, however, to keep the questions and comments in this interaction on-point. Questions posed to the student must be instructional and may be used to assess or reinforce learning. For example, you may ask the student questions that recall information, that test for understanding, that interpret data or that summarize what has been learned.

You can continue the lesson and shift to a student-centered instruction set by using the stimulus variation facilitated by student-student interaction. In this mode you redirect student questions to other students for comment or clarification. You may also ask one student to explain something to another student, thus encouraging student-student interaction.

During an instructional set, the deliberate patterning of these interaction styles, as the flow of the lesson dictates, can provide enough stimulus variation to maintain a high level of student attention and involvement in the learning experience.

4. Pausing

It is not uncommon to observe that many beginning teachers are afraid of silence during instruction. In fact, silence can be uncomfortable for most people. Effective teachers, however, understand that silence, from a dramatic pause to an extended period, can serve pedagogical functions during the teaching-learning experience. Using silence as a form of stimulus variation can be effective in several ways.

1. Silence can capture attention by contrasting sound with silence (alternating two contrasting stimuli). Attention tends to be maintained at higher levels when stimuli are varied, more so than merely increasing the intensity of a single stimulus.

2. Silence can be a signal for students to prepare for the next teacher action.

3. Silence can be used to emphasize or underscore an important point.

4. Silence can provide students time for thinking about a question or formulating an answer.

5. Silence can keep the instructor from unconsciously dominating discussion by making space and opportunity for student responses.

6. Silence can aid the instructor in listening to individual student responses

7. Silence can create suspense or expectation, thereby raising attentional states on the part of the listeners.

8. Silence can help set a focused tone for the instructional set as well as provide a model for listening behavior for other students.

9. Silence can, as a non-instructional function, demonstrate teacher disapproval of undesired student behavior.

5. Shifting Senses

Learning does not reside exclusively in the cognitive domain. Effective instructors strive to use all sensory modalities—seeing, touching, smelling, tasting, and hearing—to gain attention, maintain attention, and to help make learning "sticky." Research shows that using multiple modes of information processing helps students' ability to absorb and process information. It remains true, however, that during instructional sets about seventy percent of information consists of teacher talk. Second to verbal communication is written communication, in the form of reading texts or student writing.

Summary

Effective instructors use a wider repertoire of student senses when using stimulus variation. This wider range not only aids in maintaining attention, but also to reinforce learning by using visual, aural, kinesthetic, hearing, and tactile experiences to acquire concepts, interpret information and experiences, and to aid in retention.

❖

Chapter 9

How To Teach A Concept

There is a notion in education that states, "Anyone is able to understanding anything at some level." To one extent that is true when it comes to instruction: you can teach anyone a concept at their level. Regardless of the content (a concept, principle, or skill) anyone can learn it to some extent appropriate to their level. This means that children, adolescents, and adults of all ages can learn the same concept or principle, no matter how abstract or complex. The effective instructor can make decisions about the level of understanding each of those groups of learners can appropriately master. Sometimes you may want to merely introduce an accurate but sufficient comprehension of a concept, for example. The simplest level of understanding a concept is to recognize it ("Can you identify it?"). Often you will want to design your instruction to move a student from a naïve understanding of a concept to a more critical and nuanced comprehension.

A basic definition of a concept is: "an abstract generic idea." Because concepts are abstract ideas, they are hard to attain. However, concepts are important in learning because one fundamental and on-going work of the brain is the attainment and construction of concepts in order to make connections, achieve understanding, and to make meaning. Additionally, concept-attainment is an important component of any discipline, from engineering to faith education, because the "stuff" that makes up fields of study, disciplines, and faith, consists of concepts.

For the purpose of illustration we'll us religious studies as the focus of content, but the pedagogy of teaching concepts described here applies to any subject or field of study. Read the following list of words: Christian, Love, Salvation, Grace, Pastor, Peace, Death, Life, Justification, Faith, Teacher, Sin, Hope, Love, Eternity, Redemption, Joy, Truth, Disciple, Scripture, Bible.

Those words are examples of concepts (in engineering, examples are force, stress, flow, solid, fluid, and energy). If you are in religious studies or a church teaching, you probably have taught about those concepts at some point. And it is likely you will teach one of those concepts, or a similar one, during the week, in Sunday School, from the pulpit, in a Bible study, a small study group, or a class. Concepts are abstract and difficult to attain, but they comprise the "stuff" of faith. Therefore, it becomes important to know what a concept is, and how to teach it. When you read through the list of words did you recognize them as concepts, or as just words, objects, or topics?

Even though concepts are difficult to attain, it becomes important to be able to teach concepts to students of any age. Understanding the concept of "grace," "love," and "Christian" is as important for children as for adults. Interestingly, the cognitive attainment of concepts is the same whether a student is a kindergartner or a Ph.D. candidate. The difference lies in the degree of complexity and depth of understanding each is capable of attaining.

In this chapter we'll focus on the instructional skill of teaching concepts. Whether your students are elementary grade children or Ph.D. candidates, and whether you are teaching religious studies or science, you will use the same skill to help them acquire these important but abstract ideas. The key in teaching a concept to students' levels of understanding is to strive first for accuracy in understanding the concept rather than depth or comprehensiveness. Any age can understand a concept accurately regardless of how in-depth they are able to understand it.

When teaching concepts, it is important to distinguish a concept from a "theme," a topic, or fact. A fact is an independent discrete piece of information that commonly is believed to be true. Facts can be part of what is shared in a topic, but a fact is not a concept. For example, if we are teaching on the topic of the Bible, one fact is that the Bible consists of sixty-six books. Another is that the first Gospel that was written was the Gospel of Mark around the year 65 A.D. The thing about "facts" (information that is commonly held to be true) is that they can change (scholars debate the chronology of biblical events, the date of origin of biblical manuscripts, and, some Bibles contain more books in their canon than others). Concepts, however, are always true.

Concepts are more fundamental and universal than facts. A concept is one of the ways our brain organizes or categorizes things that have something in common. Our brains are constantly seeking patterns and connections. By bunching facts into categories or organizing them around concepts, the brain can make its own sense out of information and begin to understand it. The way your brain goes about making patterns of meaning is to organize things into concepts. If you encounter an object or an idea that does not "fit" into a pre-existing concept, then your mind creates a new category into which to locate the concept.

Remember that the brain thrives on connectivity. If a new object, idea, or truth does not "connect" with a pre-existing cognitive category or related concept, onto which your mind can graft it, then it won't be long before your brain considers it to be "trivia" and lets it go by "forgetting" it—no matter how important that fact or truth may be! Concepts consist of a category (class or set) and the attributes by which to tell whether or not an object or idea belongs in the category. Your mind, and that of your students, is constantly working at identifying concepts. Therefore, to help students see connections and make sense of the curriculum, it should be organized around concepts and principles.

Concepts are mental constructs. They consist of an organizing idea with certain criteria. Part of what is important about learning concepts is that they are universal and never change. Once your student acquires a concept he or she should be able to recognize it in any context, in any culture, and, it will be timeless. For example the concept of conflict is universal and timeless and has always existed history (from the beginning of history in the Garden according sacred texts, and shortly after with the first dramatic episode of sibling rivalry!). We have always had, and will always have, the concept of conflict. What changes are the examples through time, and the context in which it is manifested.

Teaching Concepts: The Technique

The principle behind teaching concepts in the instructional setting is: If concepts are taught by providing definitions, examples and non-examples, and by identifying criterial attributes, then learners are more likely to acquire complex concepts than if taught other ways. This technique is the most effective way to teach a concept in the instructional setting, and it works for any concept. Furthermore, you should use this technique every time you use a concept—whether in passing, or as the primary objective of your lesson.

Concepts consist of a category and attributes by which to tell whether or not an object belongs in the category. The category can be a "class" (such as in a taxonomy) or a "set," such as an object belonging to "a set of things." Your mind, and that of your students, is constantly working at identifying concepts. As the instructor, you must be able to identify the concepts contained in your lesson, course, or unit, treat them as concepts, and teach them as concepts. To pass over a concept and not follow the instructional procedure for teaching a concept runs the risk leaving students with a "vague notion" of what is being studied, or worse, of creating a misunderstanding in the mind of the student. Therefore, every time you teach a concept in the instructional setting, follow this procedure:

1. Identify the concept
2. Give a definition of the concept
3. Give an example
4. Give a non-example.
5. Test for comprehension.

You can use this procedure for teaching a minor concept that is important to understand before moving on in your instruction. But you can also use this procedure as your lesson outline for one session in order to ensure concept-mastery.

Summary

Concepts provide students frameworks for meaning making. They help students understand why things have been the way they were, why they are the way they currently are, and why things work like they do. Concepts also help student quickly understand how one thing connects with another, or not. Focusing your instruction to concepts attainment aligns with how your student's brain seeks out patterns and strives to make connections between new learning and previous knowledge and experiences. The challenge for the instructor is that if the student is not able to very quickly see a connection between new learning and their existing schemas, categories, and concepts, they tend to become confused, stop paying attention, and have difficulty in making meaning of what you are trying to teach. Use the technique for teaching a concept consistently to help bring about meaningful learning, comprehension, and retention.

❖

Chapter 10

How To Teach A Principle

Next to helping students acquire deep understanding of concepts, the most important thing instructors can achieve in the learning experience is helping students acquire and understand principles. A principle is a fundamental truth, law, doctrine, or motivating force upon which others are based. In certain fields it is an essential element or quality that produces a specific effect or explains a phenomenon.

Like concepts, and unlike facts, principles are perennial and universally true. Principles provide foundational guidelines and rules for every discipline and formal field. They are examples of "big ideas," and therefore, lead to powerful learning and meaningful application in the teaching-learning experience. Principles can further be differentiated as law-like-principles and rule-oriented-principles.

Related to our study of effective instruction, here are two examples of principles related to teaching:

1. If a teacher uses the correct technique for asking a question in the instructional setting, then learning is enhanced.

2. If a teacher uses vagueness terms when lecturing, the lack of specificity will cause confusion in the learner, thereby inhibiting learning.

Note the way the above statements are structures using the causal contingency ordering of "If . . . then." This format is used to highlight that principles are causal in the way they describe fundamental rules. If one condition is true, then the other follows.

The following are non-examples of principles:

1. When teaching the Bible the teacher should use the RSV version as often as possible. Why this is not a principle: it is non-causal; it is an opinion or preference.

2. Corporate prayers in the worship service are characterized by the use of the first person plural. Why this is not a principle: by definition this is false, it has no causality, it is not a rule. The use of the passive voice makes this a vague statement.

3. Using audio-visuals in a class presentation will make for a more effective learning experience. Why this is not a principle: it is not overtly causal, it identifies no conditions or qualifications as to what makes the use of audio-visuals effective, it is not universality true.

Here are two examples of how to state the principle behind teaching principles in the form of a principle:

1. If the teacher explains and analyses causal conditions and their effects, then students are more likely to comprehend cause-effect relationships.

2. If the teacher uses linking words to connect the conditional part of the principle to the consequent part, then the student's ability to understand and explain the principle will be higher than when the teacher just uses conjunctions ("and") or no linking words.

Here, then, is the most effective technique when teaching principles in the instructional setting:

1. **State the (causal) principle using linking words to connect effect(s) and cause(s).** Use the stronger connecting words and format "If . . . then . . ." rather than weaker connective words, like "and," in order to highlight the causal nature of the principle.

2. **Explicate the cause.** Identify and analyze the cause(s) or performance, then help students in the analysis of the cause(s). In this step, however, the instructor must watch for logical errors and cultivate critical thinking. For example, watch for occasions when students provide anthropomorphic explanations (like assigning agency to inanimate objects). Watch for and provide correction to teleological explanations in which the students use the end to describe the cause or rationale. Watch for instances in which students use normative explanations ("Because it's the law.") rather than give evidence of analysis of cause and causal dynamics. Finally, help students apply critical thinking when they substitute a reason or explanation for a cause.

3. **Explicate the effect.** In the third step the instructor leads students to identify and analyze the effect of condition then direct students to analyze the effect (the ". . . then" part of the statement of principle).

4. **Apply a causal principle.** This repertoire for learning principle reinforces understanding and retention. Apply the causal principle by leading the students in using the principle to solve a problem or to explain a known effect.

Summary

Next to concepts principles comprise the most important focus of instruction. Even when the focus of instruction and its outcome is a skill, understanding the underlying principles of that skill will help the student acquire deep understanding and proficiency. Principles help students not only understand "what" and "how," but also "why." Principles provide foundational guidelines and rules for every discipline and formal field. Because they are perennial and universally true, principles are examples of "big ideas," and therefore, lead to powerful learning and meaningful application in the teaching-learning experience. Principles can further be differentiated as law-like-principles and rule-oriented-principles.

❖

Chapter 11

How to End Instruction

In a previous chapter we likened the instructional practice of induction to how the writers of TV shows introduce the narrative and plot of each episode. We reviewed how induction is a powerful teaching and learning behavior that gets the students' attention and "sets" the brain to help it understand what it is about to learn. When you use induction learners know what to pay attention to and gain a framework upon which to acquire new learning.

In the same way, closure is the instructional practice that bookends the experience of instruction. Induction brings learners into the learning experience, and closure provides a way to end the instructional set—whether a lesson, a unit, or a course. Closure does not only provide a level of satisfaction to a learning experience, it is an important pedagogical element to effective instruction.

Again, notice how effectively writers of TV shows and movies use closure to bring your favorite weekly show to a satisfying close, or, to end a movie. Think how dissatisfied you would be not knowing what happens at the end of even one episode of your favorite show: does the criminal get caught? Is justice served to a wrongdoer? Does the boy get the girl, or vice versa? Even unresolved secondary plot lines leave us unsettled. When an episode or movie does not tie up all the loose ends of interweaving plot lines we get confused, frustrated, and dissatisfied.

Effective instructors understand this also happens in the experience of instruction. Your students feel similarly with the learning experience in the instructional setting. The final of the nine instructional skills we must master is closure. As we will see, it's more than merely a question of satisfaction, it is an integral part of the instructional arc.

Closure refers to those actions or statements by teachers that are designed to bring an instructional set—a lesson, lecture presentation, unit, or course—to an appropriate conclusion. As instructors we use closure to help students bring things together in their own minds, to make sense out of what has been going on during the course of the presentation, and to help retention.

It is accurate to consider closure as a necessary complement of set induction. If set induction is an initiating activity of the teacher, then closure is a culminating activity. Learning increases when instructors help students organize the information presented to them and to perceive relationships based on that information—from the beginning of the instructional set to end.

As an intentional part of the instructional repertoire, closure helps ensure that several critical elements in the teaching-learning experience happen. First, intentionally planning your closure segment provides you an opportunity to loop back to your learning objectives and ensure they have become learning outcomes. Second, closure helps you to better plan the scope and flow of your lesson. Third, closure helps you create ways for your students to better retain the content of instruction.

The Pedagogical Functions of Closure

Has this ever happened to you? You are listening to a presentation, a lecture in a classroom or a sermon during a Sunday morning worship service. You are well into the delivery and you hear the preacher or lecturer say, "…and in conclusion…" You notice that your brain perks up and refocuses your attention in a different way. With those words, the speaker has cued your brain that "closure" is about to happen. With renewed attentiveness, you focus on what the speaker is saying with expectancy. But then something happens. Instead of actually concluding, the speaker seems to go on with the sermon or lecture.

First, you get confused (is this the end or is there more?), then, you start getting frustrated and impatient. As you look around the room you notice signs that others in the room have started to disengage from the speaker. They are gathering their material in order to leave, some are looking away, others are checking their phones, and some have a look of impatience. You notice that the "cough index" in the room has increased. As you note these things you become aware that you are no longer paying attention to the speaker as your focus has shifted elsewhere. More significantly, you may realize that your recall of everything the speaker has said previously in the sermon or lecture is now all but forgotten.

Unfortunately, closure is too often neglected and underappreciated, when, in fact, it is a necessary component of the instructional set. Closure provides several important pedagogical functions in the teaching-learning process. Effective instruction requires intentional sequencing of the learning experience as part of instructional design.

The first pedagogical function of closure is to alert the students' attention to the end of a lesson or lesson segment. Using closure allows you to cue students to the fact that they have reached an important point in the learning process and that the instructional experience is moving toward an important segment that requires attention and response. You should plan for closure as part of the instructional arc and the student learning experience just as carefully as you did for set induction. Obviously, this means that time management becomes an important part of your instruction. You need to be aware of the time and must ensure that the end of your instruction ends with the closure set.

Simply alerting students' attention to the lesson's conclusion is not sufficient, however. The second pedagogical function of closure is to reinforce the cognitive organization of learning for students. Your lesson covered a great deal of information and your students engaged in a number of activities intended to illustrate, reinforce, integrate, manipulate, and retain the material you want them to learn. Closure can help tie it all together into a meaningful whole. Remember, in order for students to retain new learning it must be meaningful and must integrate with what has been previously learned, or, with students' experiences. Like a TV viewer, your student should not be left with a feeling of incompleteness and frustration. Similar to the end of a good episode of a detective show, students need an explanation of how the various pieces of the puzzle form a coherent picture. An effective instructor uses closure to recapitulate the various elements of the learning experience to help students gain a meaningful and coherent picture of the learning experience.

Finally, the third pedagogical function of closure is to consolidate and reinforce the major points to be learned. Once you signal the end of the lesson and provide a means to organize what was learned, you should briefly review the key concepts or processes covered in the lesson. The purpose of this function is to help students retain what they have learned in order to facilitate recall and application. Research demonstrates students tend to retain most the information presented at the beginning of the lesson and at the conclusion of the learning experience. The third function of closure includes providing students the opportunity for feedback and review.

Closure is the instructional act of helping students review the key concepts learned, of tying them together into a coherent whole (a schema or framework that provides meaning), and, of reinforcing retention by anchoring what was learned in the student's larger conceptual network.

When to Use Closure

Closure reinforces two critical functions in the teaching-learning process: review and practice, both of which aid in the retention of learning. When using review as part of closure you provide students with an opportunity to organize and place in perspective they key concepts, ideas, or skills they have learned. Practice provides students an opportunity to apply what they have learned in familiar or in new and novel situations.

Use closure at the points of the instructional arc to (1) control the discourse, (2) make transitional points overt, and (3) reinforce teaching-learning dynamics that increase attention and retention. The function of both set induction and closure techniques is to control the discourse and help make the process of instruction clear and understandable to students. In this way, students are more likely to maintain attention and retain what they have learned.

Closure can be used for numerous functions and at different times in the course of an instructional set, not just at the final conclusion of a lesson. Here are several ways you can apply closure during the arc of the instructional set:

Use closure at the end a long unit of student work

Use closure to reinforce learning of a new concept or principle through review

Use closure to close a discussion segment of a lesson

Use closure to concluded a skill-building or skill-practice activity

Use closure to end a question-and-answer session

Use closure to reinforce the presentation of a guest speaker, or of a video segment

Use closure to re-organize thinking about a new concept or principle learned.

Use closure to end a class.

Just as there are a variety of induction actions at your disposal, there are two basic types of closures you can use in your instructional repertoire. Depending on what you are teaching and at what point you are in the instructional arc, you may combine different types of closure functions and behaviors. The two types of closure are (1) review and, (2) transfer.

1. Review Closure

You will use review closure when you want to draw students' attention to a closing point in the lesson, review major points of your instructional presentation, review the sequence of learning you used in the instructional presentation, provide a summary of a student-oriented discussion, or relate the content of the lesson to an organizing principle or concept.

Review closure is appropriate when you want to help students organize their thinking around a new concept before moving on to a new idea. Use the following techniques when applying review closure:

(1) draw attention to end of lesson with a verbal cue: "Before moving to the next part of the lesson...."

(2) review the important points of your instructional presentation: "Recall that in our presentation we identified three conditions under which the action under study is called for..."

(3) use a visual representation to review, summarize, and organize students' thinking: a chart, a mindmap, an outline.

(4) call on a student to summarize the lesson: "Susan, would you please summarize what we have covered so far and cite the three major components?"

2. Transfer Closure

The second type of closure is transfer closure. You will use this instructional act to aid in the flow of the arc of the learning experience and reinforce learning. This closure activity helps provide the pedagogical functions of (1) drawing the students' attention to a closing point in the lesson, (2) extending new knowledge from previously acquired concepts, and (3) provides students an opportunity to practice and apply what they have learned.

For example, you can use transfer closure to review a homework assignment before moving on to application of ideas newly learned in the next phase of your instructional set. In this use of transfer closure you validate the effort of the homework assignment, you review previously learned concepts, you can check for and correct misunderstandings, and you signal the transition for the transfer of learning from what has been previously learned to the new segment in the learning process.

Transfer closure is helpful when ending a skill-building activity you want students to review and transfer (apply) to a new learning activity or a new context. First, have students review the skill by describing it and identifying sequence and the criteria for success or effectiveness (this fosters analysis). Then, cue the students as to how they will apply the skill in a new context or under a new condition (this fosters transfer of learning).

Summary

Closure is the instructional act of helping students review the key concepts learned, of tying them together into a coherent whole (a schema or framework that provides meaning), and, of reinforcing retention by anchoring what was learned in the student's larger conceptual network. Effective instruction brings the lesson or course to a definitive and satisfying close for students in ways that aid understanding and retention.

Bibliography

Ambrose, Susan A., Bridges, Michael, DiPietro, Michele, Lovett, Marsha C., and Norman, Marie, K. *How Learning Works: Seven Research-Based Principles for Smart Teaching*. San Francisco: Jossey-Bass, 2010.

Bain, Ken. *What the Best College Teachers Do*. Cambridge, MA: Harvard University Press, 2004.

Barbezat, Daniel, and Bush, Mirabai. *Contemplative Practices in Higher Education: Powerful Methods to Transform Teaching and Learning*. San Francisco: Jossey-Bass, 2013.

Barkley, Elizabeth F. *Student Engagement Techniques: A Handbook for College Faculty*. San Francisco: Jossey-Bass, 2009.

Blumberg, Phyllis. *Assessing and Improving Your Teaching: Strategies and Rubrics for Faculty Growth and Student Learning*. San Francisco: Jossey-Bass, 2013.

Boice, Robert. "Quick Starters: New Faculty Who Succeed," in Theall, Michael and Jennifer Franklin, eds. *Effective Practices for Improving Teaching. New Directions for Teaching and Learning*, 48. San Francisco: Jossey-Bass, 1991: 111-120.

Cahn, Steven M. *Scholars Who Teach*. Chicago: Nelson-Hall, 1978.

Davis, Barbara Gross. *Tools for Teaching*. San Francisco: Jossey-Bass, 2009.

Galindo, Israel. *A Guide to Course Design and Assessment of Student Learning.* Educational Consultants, 2008.

Galindo, Israel. *How to Be the Best Christian Study Group Leader.* Valley Forge, PA: Judson Press, 2006.

Galindo, Israel. Myths: *Fact and Fiction About Teaching and Learning.* Educational Consultants, 2004.

Galindo, Israel. *The Craft of Christian Teaching.* Valley Forge, PA: Judson Press, 1985.

Katz, Joseph and Mildred Henry. *Turning Professors into Teachers.* Phoenix: Oryx Press, 1993.

Kolb, David A. *Experiential Learning: Experience as the Source of Learning and Development.* Englewood Cliffs, New Jersey: Prentice Hall, Inc., 1984.

Lowman, Joseph. *Mastering the Techniques of Teaching.* San Francisco: Jossey-Bass Publishers, 1995.

McKeachie, Wilbert J. *Teaching Tips: Strategies, Research, and Theory for College and University Teachers.* 12th edition. Boston: Houghton Mifflin, 2006.

Nilson, Linda B. Teaching at Its Best: *A Research-Based Resource for College Instructors. San Francisco*: Jossey-Bass, 2010.

Schwartz, Barry, and Daniel Reisberg. *Learning and Memory.* New York: W. W. Norton and Company, 1991: especially, 251ff.

Wittrock, Merlin C. *Handbook of Research on Teaching,* Third Edition. New York: Macmillan Publishing Company, 1986.

Made in the
USA
Middletown, DE